ASSESSING NEEDS AND PLANNING
CARE IN SOCIAL WORK

Assessing Needs and Planning Care in Social Work

Brian J. Taylor
Assistant Principal Social Worker (Training)
Northern Health and Social Services Board
Northern Ireland

Toni Devine
Lecturer in Social Care
North West Institute of Further
and Higher Education
Londonderry

ASHGATE

361.3 TAY
151671

Published by
Ashgate Publishing Limited
Gower House
Croft Road
Aldershot
Hants GU11 3HR
England

Ashgate Publishing Company
Suite 420, 101 Cherry Street
Burlington, VT 05401-4405 USA

Ashgate website:http://www.ashgate.com

Reprinted 1994, 1995, 1998, 2002, 2004, 2005

British Library Cataloguing in Publication Data
Taylor, Brian J.
   Assessing Needs and Planning Care
   in Social Work
   I. Title II. Devine, Toni
   361.3

ISBN 1 85742 139 6 (Hbk)
ISBN 1 85742 144 2 (Pbk)

Printed and bound in Great Britain by MPG Books Ltd, Bodmin, Cornwall

Contents

List of figures

List of tables

List of examples

Acknowledgements

We would like to thank our families for their forbearance with this venture. We are grateful to our colleagues – students, managers and trainers – for contributing to the development of this text. We are particularly grateful to staff in the following organisations for sharing their practice with us:

Northern Health and Social Services Board
Western Health and Social Services Board
Eastern Health and Social Services Board
Southern Health and Social Services Board
Save the Children Fund
Salvation Army
Catholic Family Care Society
Barnardo's

Finally, special thanks to the secretaries who uncomplainingly typed and re-typed this manuscript: Mrs Helen Adams and Miss Siobhan Francis, and also to Mrs Sue Gamble who helped.

Introduction

The aim of this book is to assist readers in developing skills in caring for people – helping them to tackle problems, to learn, to grow, to cope or to change. The focus is on the social work skills required for assessing needs and planning care within a wide variety of practice situations. The book is written in the context of the Community Care systems in the UK (Griffiths, 1988; SSI, 1991a), but the focus on practice skills means that the book is applicable within a wide variety of organisational contexts throughout the world.

Even though systems vary, our key concepts remain:

- Assessment of needs and strengths
- Planning care to meet needs
- Multi-disciplinary working
- Monitoring care to ensure a quality service
- Evaluation of care provision
- Management systems to support staff and develop services.

We see this book as particularly useful to students undertaking qualifying training in social work, but it will also be of value to staff undertaking NVQ qualifications in social and health care. Our premise is that professionals are responsible for assessing needs and planning care, but that other staff will also need skills in contributing to assessment and care planning.

This book has grown out of our joint teaching on a

professional training course in social work. Our students have come from work with a range of client groups, and from day care, fieldwork and residential settings. We have drawn our examples (with their consent) from their work in family and child care, mental health, learning disability (mental handicap), physical disability and with elderly people. Here we write about a process which is fundamental to helping another person. That process is not tied to any particular setting although clearly the environment will influence practice. We write about a basic approach, not a particular set of forms to complete. The examples are to illustrate some ways in which the concepts may be applied effectively in practice. They are not put forward as perfect models or as the only way to work.

The potential scope of our subject matter is very broad. We have, therefore, imposed strict limits. First, we focus on the overall process of assessment and care planning. In our teaching programme on skills of working with individuals, a similar amount of time is given to counselling (interaction) skills, to which we refer only briefly here. There are many books available on counselling, and the reader is referred to some of these in the text.

Second, we highlight the social work process across residential, day care and fieldwork settings. This is in keeping with current developments in service delivery where staff are working across such boundaries. Our third focus is on individual care, while recognising social work as an activity which also includes groupwork and the provision of physical care.

A few terms employed need some comment. The person providing help is usually referred to as the 'social worker', though depending on the context the terms 'worker', 'counsellor' or 'helper' may also be used. 'Social worker' is never used to make a distinction between a fieldworker and a residential or day care worker. 'Social work' and 'Social Services' are used fairly interchangeably. We tend to refer to the profession as 'social work' and to the statutory employing bodies as 'Social Services', although we recognise that in Scotland and the Republic of Ireland, these statutory bodies are called 'Social Work Departments'.

The term 'client' refers to the person receiving help. This does not imply a person who is simply 'done unto', but one who is seeking help and utilising that help. The parallel is with a person utilising legal assistance, where the term 'client' is also common. Finally we avoid repetitious use of the cumbersome 'he or she' and 'he/she', by using 'he' in the main text, and 'she' in the examples, unless the context is gender specific.

Despite the fact that this book is rooted in our work with students over the years, we believe this publication is particularly timely. Changes in patterns of providing personal social services increasingly require attention to individuals, transcending demarcations between institutions and work settings. In terms of policy, the development of care in the community (Griffiths, 1988) identifies the centrality of assessing the needs of individuals, and matching services to their needs (*NHS and Community Care Act*, 1990; *People First*, DHSS, (NI), 1990). In terms of skills, we utilise the same framework in conceptualising the social work process as that used in the definition of competence of a newly qualified social worker in the UK (CCETSW 1989).

Any change in practice which you intend to implement as an employee of an organisation has implications for others. We suggest, therefore, that you need support for yourself to implement any new approach. We have included in the final chapter some pointers towards developing practice in staff teams, including residential homes and day centres. Organisational change across whole departments is beyond the scope of this book.

Finally, we recognise the contribution which you, the reader, may make to the development of practice in this area. Contributions and comments would be welome, and should be sent to:

Mr Brian Taylor
c/o Arena
Ashgate Publishing Limited
Gower House
Croft Road
Aldershot
Hants GU11 3HR
England

1 Basic principles

1.1 The basic helping cycle

It would be neat to begin with a definition of social work. Unfortunately, no agreed definition exists; as with many other professions we take it for granted. We write here about the basic process of one human being helping another. We write about 'personal' helping, though this can mean providing and giving physical care, teaching skills of everyday living, or tackling a problem with someone in distress.

Not everyone has a natural aptitude for this type of work, yet a willing person's ability to help others can be improved through training. What is effective and efficient helping? What skills are required? These questions introduce the need for a theory, or model of helping, to clarify what working in social situations really means for both client and worker.

Many theories about social work practice exist. Some of the most important are mentioned in Chapter 4. Most useful theories focus on the *interaction* between the client and the worker, whether this is in individual counselling, work with groups, or in practical care of some kind. We accept this emphasis, but recognise that social work operates within a context. Most workers seeking to develop their social work skills are employees in an agency. In other words, the social worker is helping someone not just as a friend, a neighbour or even an autonomous counsellor would do. The help provided by the

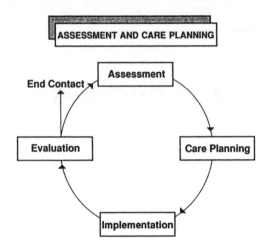

Figure 1.1   The basic helping cycle

worker is supported and constrained by laws, policies, procedures, and some system of accountability to the wider society. The worker has colleagues within his own organisation and other organisations (such as housing and health agencies) with whom he must form working relationships. There are records to keep and reports to write. Increasingly there is business planning, service contracts and the setting of quality objectives. The organisations change along with their services, greater accountability may be required in relation to use of resources, and demands are made for higher standards of practice. The worker in the social agency, trying to serve his client, works within the context of changing values, be they personal (worker and client), professional, organisational, or societal.

The 'basic helping cycle', as explained here, represents a systematic way of looking at social work practice in a value-based context. Its application is broad enough to encompass a variety of personal services including counselling, providing care for residents of homes, and teaching in developmental programmes for day centre members. The model (Figure 1.1) has inherent logic without a prescriptive format, assisting the social worker in providing useful services to a greater or lesser depth, depending on circumstances. As a model for practice, it allows for the 'use of self' – your own personal skills and attributes which are so essential – while also accounting for the use of resources to managers.

Assessment, planning, implementation, and evaluation are the four building blocks of the helping cycle. Subsequent chapters define these words in greater detail, but listed here are meanings close to their everyday usage:

Assessment: What is the problem? What needs to be learnt?
               What are the strengths and limitations in this
               situation?
Planning: What should be done about it? By whom?
Implementation: Let's get into action!
Evaluation: How are things at the finish of our efforts?

This is a model fundamental to many professions. Similar processes are outlined for management (Jaycees, 1974), education (Hunt and Hitchin, 1986), nursing (Yura and Walsh, 1979), psychiatric nursing (Ward, 1985), youth work (Jardine, 1987), and young offenders work (Pickles, 1987). In social work, variants are applied such as in mental handicap (Brechin and Swain, 1987) and cystic fibrosis (Spastics Society, 1987).

The purpose here is to demonstrate the application of this basic problem-solving cycle to social work with a range of client groups in a variety of settings. Throughout the book, a dual focus is maintained on both client and agency, with the worker as mediator between these (Shulman, 1992). Figure 1.2 outlines the process steps taken by the client and the agency; the cycle has been drawn as a straight-line sequence for clarity. Figure 1.3 shows the cycle with its four main phases, including in each phase the major components of practical action.

1.2   Social work skills and values

How can we define something dynamic in static words? That is the difficulty in describing the helping process. Boxes and demarcation lines are used to capture a process which essentially is flowing. Social work is seldom, if ever, a neat and

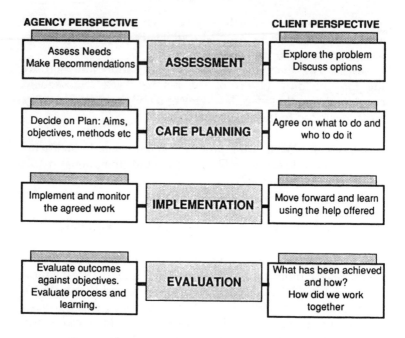

AGENCY PERSPECTIVE   **CLIENT PERSPECTIVE**

| Assess Needs Make Recommendations | **ASSESSMENT** | Explore the problem Discuss options |

| Decide on Plan: Aims, objectives, methods etc | **CARE PLANNING** | Agree on what to do and who to do it |

| Implement and monitor the agreed work | **IMPLEMENTATION** | Move forward and learn using the help offered |

| Evaluate outcomes against objectives. Evaluate process and learning. | **EVALUATION** | What has been achieved and how? How did we work together |

Figure 1.2   Client and agency perspectives

orderly process from start to finish; it is an *art*, incorporating sciences, values, policies and personal skills. The practice material provided here needs to be accompanied by training and supervised experience if it is to be effective in developing your skills.

Training is essential, but that doesn't mean that techniques can be put into people. Helpers need to *grow* and develop, usually with some nurturing. They need to become less confined by their own limitations and concerns in order to listen attentively, offering others the opportunities to make decisions for themselves. Less tangible qualities such as self-awareness and personal maturity also affect the social worker's ability to help others. The *relationship* between the helper and the helped is central. It is not, however, a relationship for its own sake but one developed through the process of working together.

For the worker, this relationship with a client, is informed by

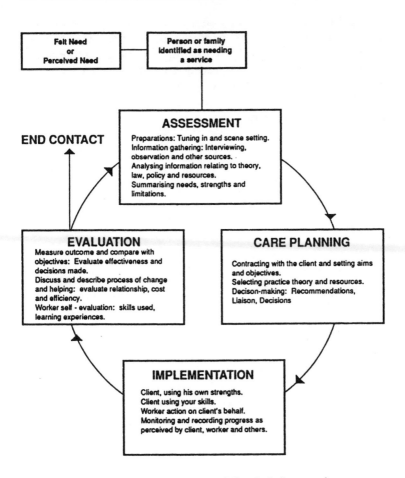

Figure 1.3 Major components of the helping cycle

health studies, social sciences, knowledge of agency policies and resources and undergirded by social work values. These *values* have largely grown with the profession, from its roots in Christian voluntary organisations and social movements of the last century. There is no universal Code of Ethics, but the basic ethical principles have stood the test of time (cf. Biestek, 1957) and are now embodied in Statements of Professional Competence (CCETSW, 1989).

Empathy with the client is essential. So many clients have their hopes hampered by handicap or distress. The helping process, however logical, is like 'an empty gong booming' unless it has at its heart a caring concern which clients can realise and recognise. People under stress or facing a new challenge need a helper who will stimulate and motivate energies and imagination.

2 Assessment

2.1 Purpose of assessment

Assessment is a tool to aid in the planning of future work, the beginning of helping another person to identify areas for growth and change. Its purpose is the identification of needs; it is never an end in itself. From an agency perspective, the object of assessment is to make possible informed decisions about meeting client needs. For the client, 'assessment' is basically discussing the current situation with the helper.

In social work, assessment includes the following elements:

- Making sense of a situation, for the client and the worker.
- Building up a picture of what happens, probable causes and probable consequences.
- Identifying problems or issues of concern to the person seeking help, areas for learning or growth.
- Relating the client and the situation to relevant organisational aspects such as law, policies, criteria for services, resources and responsibilities for risk-management.
- Identifying strengths both in the person needing help and in his situation as resources to draw upon in the work.
- Identifying some of the difficulties likely to be encountered in work towards certain goals.
- Establishing the level of existing strengths and needs as a base-line by which to measure progress.

- Beginning a process of clarifying expectations between the person receiving help and the person giving the help so that they can build an open working relationship.

Assessment is the beginning of forming an agreement or 'contract' to work on an area of need, the first step in forming a working relationship. Assessment should not be seen as a cold process of gathering information to put on to a form. The summarising of information for agency purposes is only one part of the process. A further vital element is engaging the client in a constructive relationship.

Client perspective

The assessment will normally be fully shared with the client. The client is unlikely to invest energy and enthusiasm in a process of change if he is denied information, or feels that powerful interests are acting 'behind his back'. The worker's task is to motivate the client so that outcomes are as positive as possible; this means sharing information with the client as well as respecting client priorities. Aims and priorities are normally fully agreed with clients based on the assessment.

Information sharing and full client consent are the normal approaches to social work practice. Although client consent is always sought, there are occasions when action is taken without consent of all parties, for example, for the protection of children.

In the case of compulsory intervention, it is particularly important that the worker's role is clear. The client is entitled to know the limits of the worker's power; to receive an explanation of the action that is being taken, and why; and to be involved as far as possible. The client's energies need to be directed towards productive change, within the context of the social worker's obligations under the law.

Agency perspective

For the agency, an assessment culminates in a presentation of a summary of the information gathered. The manager then must decide about allocating services (the planned care) for a particular client. This may be only the allocation of a worker's time to this client, and agreement on the aims and methods of this work, though it may equally involve the provision of other services through other staff within the agency. The client may decide at this stage to 'go it alone', or seek help from another agency. The assessing agency may also refer a client to another agency which offers more suitable assistance.

Social work agencies will normally have assessment arrangements in place with agencies providing health care, housing, and so on. There will be some system for initial assessment (screening) to decide whether a multi-disciplinary assessment is required. The screening stage ensures that only complex situations are referred for full multi-disciplinary assessment. Such complex cases are where:

1 a change of residence is required
2 services from a number of agencies need to be closely co-ordinated in order to enable the client to continue living at home.

Where a multi-disciplinary assessment is required, one professional will be nominated to co-ordinate the care plan. It is important to separate this 'care management' role (which may be carried by a social worker or by another professional) from the distinctive social work contribution to a multi-disciplinary assessment.

A popular format for decision making in social work organisations is the 'review', a combination of an assessment of current information with an evaluation of work already undertaken with the client. This is illustrated in Figure 2.1. The review

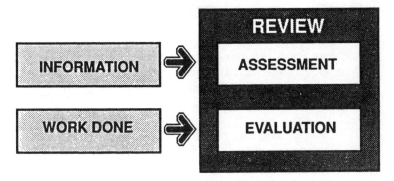

Figure 2.1 Assessment as part of an agency review

normally involves the client, although sometimes clients attend only part of review meetings.

From the point of view of the social worker, the assessment process can be divided into two parts, the gathering of information and the analysing of information, as illustrated in Figure 2.2.

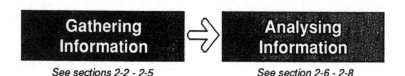

Gathering Information	⇨	**Analysing Information**
See sections 2-2 - 2-5		*See section 2-6 - 2-8*

Figure 2.2   Phases of assessment

What is required in assessment is a summarising and interpretation of information useful to both the client and the agency. There are few absolutes about any situation, and no

---

Example: Aims of assessment

Andrews family referred to family centre
Reason for referral: To assess the possibility of the children returning home to their mother.
Areas of work:
  1   Assess bonding relationship between mother and children
  2   Assess relationship between co-habitee and children
  3   Assess parenting skills of the two adults

foolproof predictors of the outcome of possible helping strategies. Nonetheless, assessments should be:

- reliable (they can be repeated)
- efficient (the outcome is worth the resources used)
- valid (they give a true picture)
- useful (they fulfill their purpose)

The assessment needs to have appropriate breadth and focus in order to be useful; global generalisations are of little use. Conversely, although there is sometimes a place for very narrow assessments and high fidelity results, this can also be limited in its usefulness. What is required is a grasp of the situation which can help in formulating a plan to develop the assets and minimise the liabilities in the situation.

2.2 Sources of information

The assessment process begins with preparing to gather information from a variety of sources, which can be grouped as follows:

1 observation
2 interviewing the client or clients
3 other sources, both people and written records.

In some areas of social work (for example, psychiatric children's units) observation is a major tool. In other areas (for example, fieldwork) interviewing is more prominent. The use of other people and written records varies considerably from one working group to another. Although the usefulness of these different sources depends on the setting, many situations would benefit from a more even balance between them.

Interviewing the client is normally the major source of information, since the client's perception of the situation has to be the basis for effective social work. The definition of 'the client' must be the one most useful for a particular situation. A family or a couple may be the focus of work rather than an individual.

The distress of an individual is often the product of interaction with others rather than a 'problem' within the individual concerned. Some forms of mental illness, for instance, can be seen as produced or compounded by the interaction of the family or living group. The theoretical basis for this is drawn from systems theory (for example Specht and Vickery 1977; Middleman and Goldberg 1974). Family therapy approaches (Chapter 4) are a particular application of systems theory to family situations, looking at such dimensions as communication patterns, roles, sub-groups or boundaries.

Even in a relatively straightforward situation, it is often helpful to complement your information with the views of others. In a day centre for mentally handicapped adults, for example, you should draw on the views of other workers. The way that John behaves with you in the education room may be quite different from the way he behaves with Michael, the instructor in the workshop. A member may demonstrate skills in the day centre, for instance, which are not used at home and this may be due either to attitudes of your client or to those of the carers. Only an assessment which includes the perceptions of all the significant people will be full enough to provide the information necessary to plan an effective programme.

At the 'screening' stage, decisions will be made about the involvement of other professions, such as the health visitor, speech therapist or community psychiatric nurse. Their contributions will normally be in the form of a written report whether or not there is an actual review meeting.

Each profession is responsible for the assessment of those areas which fall within its own competence. The co-ordination of these contributions to the assessment falls to a nominated person referred to as a 'named worker', a 'case co-ordinator' a 'case manager' or a similar title. The case co-ordinator is frequently a social worker, though it may not be. In this case, your primary role will be to co-ordinate the expertise available as well as contributing from your own professional domain.

In assessment you must first decide what information you need in order to formulate a plan of action. You will almost certainly need information about the presenting problem and the current situation and perhaps about past events. Discussions about family history ('genograms') are particularly useful

Example: Multi-disciplinary assessment

Contributing to assessment
Carnside Hospice has an extensive day care facility. Upon referral an initial assessment of need is made jointly by the doctor and social worker attached to the Hospice. The doctor sees the patient, whilst the social worker interviews the family to assess their need for respite. If a place is offered, the occupational therapist makes an assessment and plans an activity programme.

Co-ordinating assessment
Deirdre is shortly to transfer to Demesne Adolescent Hostel from Dappleford Children's Home. For the assessment of need before her independence training programme, information was sought (verbally or in written reports) from: field social worker, residential staff, Educational Welfare Officer, Educational Psychologist, Headmaster and school teacher.

in some family therapy work, but an excessive amount of family detail may be wasteful of your time. Even more importantly, it may be a waste of your client's time and detract from helping. 'If it is not pertinent, it is probably impertinent!'

Having decided what information you need, where are you going to find it? You may need to amend your plan as new information comes to light or as the situation unfolds, but you must have some logical strategy. Sometimes certain people will be the only ones to have particular items of information. On other occasions you may need the perspectives of different people about the same situation. You will need to decide on the balance of direct observation, client interviews, and information from other sources.

Begin by acquainting yourself with all the existing records within your own unit and agency to save duplication of effort, being aware of issues of confidentiality.

Example: Planned information gathering

Mrs Edwards
In preparing to draw up a comprehensive care plan for Mrs Edwards, a resident in Evenmore Home for the elderly mentally infirm, information might be gathered from:

1   existing GP and SW records
2   interviews with the consultant psychogeriatrician and clinical psychologist
3   interviews with Mrs Edwards, her married son and his wife
4   observations of other staff in the home.

Miss Frances McFadden
Sometimes the plan for information gathering (and subsequent action) has to be guided by questions such as:

• Who knows, or doesn't know?
• Who is entitled to know what?
• How would this client like to be approached?

Apply these questions to the following scenario:

Client: MISS FRANCES McFADDEN   Age: 19
From: Sister Forsythe, Maternity Unit.
Referral to social worker: No feelings for new-born baby. Is talking about possibility of adoption. Frances does not get on with her mother. No antenatal care. Family GP unaware of pregnancy.

Before going on to approach other workers or to seek records from other agencies, confidentiality needs to be carefully considered. Normally you would expect to seek the client's consent to approach other agencies or to ask for any records from them. The approach to family, friends or neighbours normally requires careful discussion with a client beforehand. In some situations, it is important to ascertain whose permission is required to approach whom. This may be required where children or people with learning disability or mental illness are involved.

The source of referral or request for assistance is an important starting point in planning the sequence of assessment. The person making the referral has a right to know how the information will be used. Unless there is a statutory obligation otherwise, the referrer has a right to control the use of the information. Where one person asks for help for another, additional factors need to be included, such as whether the referrer has informed the referee that this request has been made. As you proceed, be careful to record the sources of different items of information.

Although this wider range of sources is often important, we would like to emphasise that the most important source of information is normally the client himself.

2.3 Observation skills

It is helpful to observe your client in a variety of situations, both alone and in a group. A family setting may reveal a vast amount. Indeed, those who work in family therapy make extensive use of the interaction between family members as a central part of their work. You may find the accounts given to you by different individuals do not harmonise entirely with your own observation of events. Another benefit of observation is that you may later be able to offer a different understanding of a situation to help the client deal with it more constructively (see Figure 2.3).

Observations should normally be planned and carried out with client consent. You will want some observations which are 'detached', in which you are not part of the action but observing your client on his own or with others. You will also have 'participant' observations, records you have made during your own interaction with the client in real life situations, but sometimes it is more helpful to create structured scenarios.

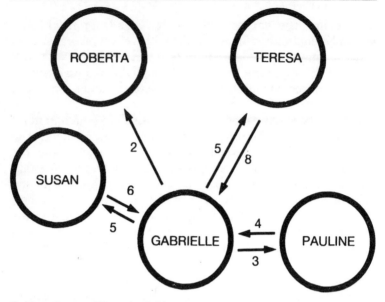

Setting: Group sitting at a table

Observation
Gabrielle has a balanced level of communication with Susan, Teresa and Pauline. Gabrielle attempts to initiate discussion with Roberta who does not reciprocate, despite sitting opposite.

Key
ⓧ = Individuals
→ = Direction of communication with number of times initiated in the time period

Figure 2.3   Sociogram used to assist in describing behaviour in a group

The value of open, honest work with clients indicates that observations should normally be fully agreed with your client in advance. However the client does not always need to know the precise moment when you are undertaking observation. If the client's behaviour would be changed by knowing that you are observing, you might seek consent in advance, agreeing that the precise timing of the observation would not be disclosed.

The observation you undertake will be guided by the needs of

Table 2.1   A guide to planning observations

Antecedents	Are there certain behaviours which occur immediately before the behaviour in question? Are there factors which are present which seem to have a bearing on it?
Behaviour	You can ask yourself the classic questions about a particular behaviour: Where? When? What? Who? How?
Consequences	What else happens as a consequence of the behaviour in question? What is the effect of having such a consequence following the previous behaviour? How significant are these in influencing ('rewarding') the behaviour in question? How does the consequence feel to the client?

Example: Identifying precipitating factors

Mrs Irvine, aged 73, receiving care at home
According to her daughter, Mrs Irvine began to show lack of interest in her life and home when her son returned home from Canada after 20 years. He had quickly decided that he could not stay with his mother due to the ever-present threat of violence from terrorists, and the high profile of the police and army in the locality. She had been very upset that her son would not stay with her during his visit, and her loss of motivation seemed to stem from that time.

the client and the approaches to the work you may later undertake. For example, a schedule for analysing client need

Example: Patterns of behaviour – some recurrent behaviours

Mrs Harris, aged 75, in a residential home

Chart to show number of occurrences in a 30 minute observation period	1 Dining Room	2 Lounge	3 At Day Care Activity
Interaction Conversation with staff with wide smiling and grinning	5	3	4
Body Frozen stance, devoid of all movement for 3–5 seconds	3	2	0
Speech Rhetorical repetition of words and topics of conversation with inappropriate manner	3	6	3

might be a useful guide to setting up a series of observations. An alternative possibility is to observe aspects of the 'problem', such as extent, duration, intensity, and urgency of the issues that cause concern.

One approach to planning observations can be derived from behavioural theory (see Table 2.1). Another guide to planning and carrying out observations comes from the psychology of interpersonal behaviour, and social skills training (see Argyle, 1972 and 1988; Morris, 1977; Pease, 1981) (Table 2.2).

Table 2.2 Non-verbal cues

Voice	Tone, volume, emotional content speed, hesitations accent, style language, phraseology and jargon
Facial	Eye contact Facial gestures
Body	Position Posture Hand and other gestures Proximity Use of touch

In reviewing your observations, seek to identify behaviours which recur in a variety of different situations and those which recur in the same sequence on separate occasions (patterns of behaviour).

A key factor at this stage is the ability to separate fact from interpretation. Your own presence in the situation may change the behaviour you observe and it is not possible to prevent this. Sometimes client behaviour may improve through the extra attention of the assessment process, without any strategy for development being implemented! If you think that your presence may have influenced what you have observed, try to record what influence you think you have had on the situation. Also, ask the client or others what influence they think your behaviour has had.

2.4 Preparation for interviews

Effective interviews require effective preparation. Good preparation shows concern for your client and helps clients to feel valued.

Tuning-in

'Tuning-in' can be likened to adjusting the dial of a radio to obtain the best reception. It is the mental preparation that the social worker undertakes to prepare himself for the matters which the client may wish to discuss.

This tuning-in must be at a feeling level, not merely an intellectual process and it may be helpful to recall experiences similar to those of the client. The client's feelings may relate to his circumstances, to a particular difficulty, to yourself as an authority figure, or perhaps to some features of the institution or agency within which you work.

Tuning-in can be seen in terms of different levels. A first level would be to the general category of the client: what is it like to be an elderly person or an adolescent? Experience can be complemented by reading about the stages of physical, emotional and social development. As well as the standard texts on psychology and human development, there are many books about social work with specific groups which might be helpful, and also autobiographies by people with particular needs.

The second level of tuning-in would be to this specific client or clients. What do you already know about this person, from the agency records, from the referral or reason for undertaking the assessment? What do you already know about the relationships within the family or with other neighbours or workers?

The third level of tuning-in would relate to the specific phase of work. You may be meeting this person for the first time. How is he likely to feel about this meeting? Is he likely to be afraid of new demands? What sense of hope or aspiration is he likely to have? This tuning-in is undertaken before each contact with the client. In later interviews, some of the concerns will change. As the relationship develops this aspect of the tuning-in changes considerably.

A key element in tuning-in to the client is an awareness of ambivalence. This simply means awareness that, although a person would like to change, there is also a fear or guardedness about the demands that this will make. The worker needs to be aware of both aspects. An over-emphasis on possible resistance to help can lead to a self-fulfilling prophesy that the client does

---

Example: Tuning-in

I sat myself down in the sitting room of the home for half an hour in the position in which Mrs Jackson sits, in order to see the world from her view. The position maintained is painful, and I don't have osteo-arthritis. Mrs Jackson can do little but think, so I thought about being parted from the sister I'm closest to, how it would feel especially if I'd looked after her and her family all her life – rejection, anger, helplessness, making excuses for fear I'd lose her altogether.

---

not really want help anyway. On the other hand, the worker's awareness of the client's desire for help and potential for change should not become a blindness to genuine fears.

Finally the worker needs to tune in to himself. How are you feeling as you approach this session? It may be that you have some anxieties because of the type of work, or because of what you know of this client. If you have such feelings but do not become aware of them before the session, they may arise during the session and your mind may become distracted. By tuning-in to your own feelings and experiencing them before the session with the client, you can reduce their power to block your helping.

Occasionally a new worker is wary of making extensive preparations for fear of prejudicing the work. Will I do the client a disservice by not allowing him 'a new start'?

Good preparation, however, will avoid the danger of inappropriate action and the time-wasting of asking clients to repeat matters already discussed, and assist in focusing the work. You need not accept the perceptions of others as gospel truth, but having understood how another worker or person sees a situation, you can be better prepared for the client's attitude to that person. This may alert you to approaches which have been

---

Example: Tuning-in to yourself

Tuning-in to myself raises issues about my ability to handle Mrs Jackson's grief. I believe that people have a right to the truth about their illness, its prognosis and implications. Will I be able to avoid colluding with Mrs Jackson's denial of reality without destroying her? I must remember not to be impatient for results.

This is not my problem and not my solution. It is Mrs Jackson's, so go at her pace.

I am afraid of failing – of failing Mrs Jackson and of failing at my work.

---

particularly successful or markedly unsuccessful before you undertake your own action.

Scene setting

The setting in which you speak to the client will influence how relaxed, how alert, and how responsive the client is. Is the room warm enough, and is it comfortable? Are lighting and ventilation adequate? What are the seating arrangements like? Are they suitable for the type of work which you have in mind? In general, easy chairs at an angle to each other are recommended for counselling situations. Chairs side by side make it more difficult to observe non-verbal cues, or to attend sufficiently to what the other person is saying. Chairs which directly face each other can be more formal, or alternatively more intimate. The positioning of desks and tables can also help or hinder the work.

Thought also needs to be given to the privacy of the situation. What do you need to do to avoid disturbances from the telephone or from people knocking at the door? Is the room sufficiently soundproof to prevent others overhearing and to keep out outside noise? Finally, are you equipped with the information (papers?) required for the session?

Example: Scene setting

I had met with Mrs Jackson in the small sitting room of the home. When I arrived she was sitting in an easy chair and appeared comfortable and relaxed. I sat on a low stool in front of her so that she could see my face and we could have eye contact.

You should also consider risks to your own safety in particular situations. Do you have adequate support and other emergency devices? If you are interviewing the client in his own home, does someone at the office know where you are? Will someone notice your absence if you do not return on time?

2.5 Interviewing skills

Good interviewing is a practical way of putting into effect social work values, such as:

- genuine interest and caring;
- respect for the person as an individual with opinions, feelings and skills; and
- a willingness to communicate honestly and yet compassionately.

Structure

The skills and values enshrined in social work, as discussed in the two previous sections, apply to the overall process of helping others in a professional context. The helping cycle also applies to each event or individual session with clients. Assessment, planning, implementation and evaluation skills are called for in every phase of the process. Individual sessions with clients have preparations, beginnings, middles and ends, just as the overall helping intervention does (see Figure 2.4).

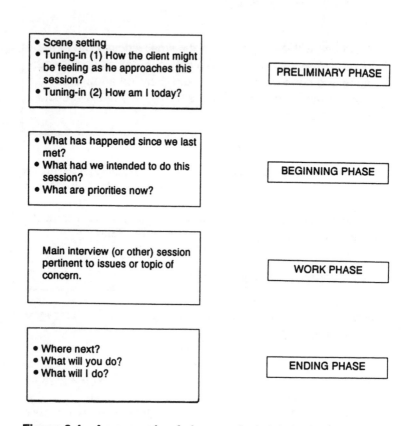

Figure 2.4   An example of phases of work in a single session

The amount of time devoted to each phase of the helping cycle varies from one session to another. Typically the amount of preparation required is greater in the earliest sessions as the worker and client 'come to terms with each other', identifying and agreeing the work to be done. In the planning and implementation phases, the pattern of working may be well established, requiring only a few minutes in 'beginnings' and a few minutes at the end to tie things up. As the intervention

Assessment and Care planning	Implementation	Evaluation

2–4 weeks (approximately) Move on when contract for work agreed

8–12 weeks (approximately) Move to close: at agreed time

1–2 weeks

Figure 2.5   Time-scale for short-term work

draws to a close, more time will inevitably be spent on ending-phase aspects.

There are no hard and fast rules about how long a period of helping should take, either for individual sessions or for the overall process, which may stretch to many sessions. Similarly, there is no set time-scale for any part of the helping cycle. The worker will be guided by the type of work being undertaken in individual sessions, the client's concentration level and emotional energy, and inevitably by the constraints of time. Some guidance in relation to overall time-scales is available from research (Reid and Shyne, 1969; Reid and Epstein, 1977; Epstein, 1982) which led to the development of the Task Centred Casework Method. (A thorough account of this model is readily available in an earlier book from Ashgate (Doel, 1992).)

The task centred model illustrates something fundamental about human capacity to cope with stress, and to harness energies on emotional issues or personal helping. Figure 2.5 illustrates a typical pattern, or 'rule of thumb' derived from the study, and includes reference to 2 to 4 sessions to agree on the basis for work, followed by 6 to 12 sessions of counselling. Some situations may be so stressful that more frequent contact is required. Other kinds of work sessions such as teaching programmes are considerably less stressful, and may lend themselves to a longer span of time over which greater confidence and experience is gained.

Body language

Your body will convey non-verbal signals about your attitudes to the person you are with. Are these the messages of a good listener and an effective helper? Is your posture encouraging the other person to speak? Leaning forward and having an 'open' posture is often described as being helpful. Are you looking towards the person who is speaking? Does your expression convey interest in what is being said? What eye contact is appropriate? Too intense or too little eye contact are both disconcerting and unhelpful. Where appropriate, do you use touch as an aid to communication? Do your reactions convey your interest and concern for this person?

Questions

Sensitive questioning is an important area of interviewing in the assessment phase. Different types of questions have different uses.

1 *Open questions* encourage the client to express what he is thinking and feeling. They are especially useful in early phases of an interview.

   Example: 'Tell me a little about yourself'
              'What would you like us to do?'

2 *Closed questions* obtain the more precise information required for planning the work.

   Example: 'How long ago did that happen?'
              'Who else was involved?'

3 *Probing questions* are seeking to pursue a particular area, but with some openness. They are not intended to be harsh.

   Example: 'Would it be useful to talk more about that?'
              'Can you tell me more about that?'

Some types of questions are generally unhelpful. For example, leading questions give the recipient no choice of answer, as the answer is incorporated in the question. Multi-answer questions are less helpful than those with a simple response.

   Questions can help the client to make better sense of the

'emotional jungle' in which he finds himself. Your questions may help in increasing self-awareness.

Empathy

A crucial factor in the client's willingness to open up is the 'empathy' of the worker. 'Empathy' includes:

- receptivity to and acceptance of what the client is saying;
- conveying to the client that you have heard what has been said;
- conveying that you understand the feelings behind what is said;
- and assisting the client to express the feeling underlying the statements that he makes.

The client's own description of his situation is recorded as 'fact'. This does not mean that the situation would look exactly the same to yourself or to anyone else, but it is a fact that the client perceives the situation in this way. This is important for the purpose of your work with the client. It does not necessarily mean that you agree with it. You accept the client's view as being reality for him. Assessment is not 'passing judgment'.

Confrontation

We must not, on the other hand, neglect the need for confrontation at times. The client who does not acknowledge that he has any part to play in the difficult situation is unlikely to make much progress. This does not mean that change within other people in the situation may not be desirable. However helping the client to 'own' the problem is an important early step in taking strategic action.

The realities of life, or the realities of the situation may well be in contradiction to statements made by the client. Important development can be stimulated by illustrating the disparity. The need to make sense of objective fact, which has been quietly ignored, can be a turning point in a counsellee's progress.

Communication

It may sometimes be helpful to utilise non-verbal methods of communication with your client. In working with children, with adolescents, or with people with a learning disability this can be invaluable. The use of play (such as dolls, puppets, toy telephones, and so on) is often used in work with children who are suspected of being sexually abused. With any children, an activity can stimulate and assist verbal communication. For example, Life Story Books, water transferred from one container to another, or candles lit in sequence help children moving from one case situation to another.

With clients who have a learning disability there is also the potential of sign languages (such as Makaton) and signing systems (such as Paget-Gorman). (See Kiernan et al., 1982; Jones and Cregan, 1986.)

There is an interesting range of pencil-and-paper methods which are useful with a wide variety of clients. Some examples are:

- *Life line*:   a snake-like line is marked off to illustrate different ages of the client, and significant comments put against each.
- *Problem tree*:   from a circle including the client's name in the centre, lines are drawn outwards connecting areas for growth and sub-groups of these.
- *Brainstorm*:   ideas connected with a particular problem are put in random fashion on a sheet of paper.
- *Card sort*:   cards covering a range of pertinent issues are sorted by the client into groups indicating seriousness or urgency.
- *Self-perception questionnaires*:   questionnaires which can be completed to illustrate how the client sees himself or would like to see himself.

(For further examples, see Priestley et al., 1978.)

Crisis

A quite different consideration at this phase of the work is that if a client is in a state of crisis, this will have implications for his approach to the work, and consequently to your own. First, the client's feelings will be near the surface, and work cannot proceed until these have been expressed and received by the

Example: Engaging the client's family

The family welcomed me into their home and seemed very friendly. However, over a period of an hour, each time I focused discussion on the work they changed the subject to granny's health, a new sewing machine, even the soap they preferred. They said they were aware of the reason for my visit – as explained by Mandy – but they refused to give me their agreement by changing the subject.

At this stage I produced the assessment scale hoping that it would allay any fears by giving them a more concrete example of the work . . .

After numerous attempts on my part to focus the discussion Granny produced a crocheted rug which she claimed Mandy had made, as an example of her hobbies. I admired the rug. Granny then said, 'I hope you are not offended.' At first I did not understand the reference but said that I had not been offended. Granny then looked past me directly at Mandy's father and again said 'I hope you are not offended.'

I could feel a pause and a tension so I asked why I would be offended. 'By the colours of the rug' she replied. (The rug was multi-coloured) I am sure I must have looked puzzled – 'The red, white and blue' she said. The reference was to my non-British cultural and religious background. 'No I am not offended', I said, and smiled although I did feel uncomfortable. 'I do not make a difference to people', I said, 'each to their own beliefs'.

At this point Mandy's father began telling me about his beliefs and I agreed that life was about helping each other where we could. Granny then looked directly at her son and nodded. He returned the nod and she announced that they could work with me as I explained things well. I felt as if I had passed a test.

helper. Second, the client in crisis may feel out of control, and a firm and supportive worker can be of great assistance. The worker who is competent and can clarify direction can steady the client immeasurably. Third, the energy for work or change is much more intense whilst the client is in crisis (see Morrice, 1976; O'Hagan, 1986). Aspects of this are discussed below, related to motivation for change (Chapter 3).

2.6   Organising information: schedules

Information is only useful if it can be retrieved efficiently. Ideas need to be organised in a logical and helpful fashion. Schedules may be used in organising information. A very simple schedule is shown in Figure 2.6. This shows five aspects about which you

Perceptions	Client	Family	Other workers	Your own
1 Personality				
2 History				
3 Circumstances				
4 Strengths				
5 'The problem' or needs				

Figure 2.6   A simple schedule

may be gathering information. The other axis shows some of the sources you may have used to gather information. Do not feel obliged to gather information from every source about every aspect. What is important is to be aware of different sources of information about different aspects, and to seek for information from the appropriate places. It is important to record the source of the information (for example, the views of different family members about a mental health problem).

There are many sophisticated schedules available, normally designed for use with particular client groups. Some examples which are available to social workers are given in Table 2.3.

Schedules are systematically organised headings or questions based on the wisdom of experienced practitioners. In the process of information gathering, they are extremely helpful in ensuring that important aspects are not missed. However, every schedule has its limitations, quite apart from the fact that it is designed for a specific purpose which may not be the one for which you are using it. It is important therefore to remember that schedules are a tool, not a procedure to be followed slavishly. You may need two or more schedules to cover your purpose. Or you may want to supplement one main schedule with parts of another schedule or some additional headings of your own.

There may be agency requirements which affect the selection of a schedule: information provided under consistent headings, for instance, is more accessible to other staff. If staff are familiar with the schedule used, they can often understand it more quickly than a report under unfamiliar headings. Also, the allocation of resources between clients is simplified if their needs are assessed by the same range of criteria, and presented in a standard format. Thus although a personal selection of schedules might be used in an individual case, where services have to be provided to a group of clients some standardisation may be beneficial.

Schedules are valuable in guiding information gathering but their primary purpose is to help you to organise systematically the material which is the fruit of your assessment.

2.7 Theory for practice

Our focus has so far been on describing how the client functions in various situations, together with something of the background to the situation, and organising this material in some

Table 2.3   Some schedules used in social work

Children
Attachment and Separation: Fahlberg (1981)
Behaviour Scale: Rutter (1967)
Physical and Social Development in Early Years: Sheridan (1982)
Activity and Hyperactivity: Werry (1968)
Factors Related to Behaviour Problems: Lask and Lask (1981)
Children at Risk: Department of Health (1988)
'Problem' Children: Hoghughi (1980); Herbert (1981)
Child Care and the Family: A Client Management Resource Pack: M. Herbert (1991) NFER-NELSON*
Social Skills Training for Children and Adolescents: Spence (1980) NFER-NELSON
Looking After Children: Assessment and Action Records: HMSO (1991)

Family
Numerous frameworks for different practice theories. Some examples:
Family Interactions: Haley (1976)
Transactional Analysis: Pitman (1984)
Genograms: Department of Health (1988)
Family Life Cycle: Carter and McGoldrick (1981)
Parenting: Adcock and White (1985)

Children with Learning Disability
Cunningham and Sloper (1978)
Newson and Hipgrave (1982)
Portage Scheme: Bluma et al. (1976)
Family Stress: Holroyd (1974); Crnic et al. (1983)
Adaptive Behaviour Scale: Nihira et al. NFER-NELSON
Bereweeke Skill-Teaching System: Felce et al. NFER-NELSON
Behaviour Assessment Battery: Kiernan and Jones (1977) NFER-NELSON
Vineland Adaptive Behaviour Scale: Doll (1936, 1953); Sparrow et al. (1984) NFER-NELSON

continued

Table 2.3 *continued*

Adults with Learning Disability
General Assessment: Whelan and Speake (1979)
Work Skills Rating Scale: Whelan and Schlesinger (1976)
Progress Assessment Chart: Gunzberg (1969)
Learning Opportunities Co-ordination Survey: Gunzberg and Gunzberg (1987)
Effects of Disability: Gilbert (1985)
Hampshire Assessment for Living with Others: Bailey (1980)
Making a Move: Sperlinger (1990) NFER-NELSON
When Dad Died: Working Through Loss: Hollins and Sireling (1991) NFER-NELSON
Social Use of Language Programme: Rinald (1991) NFER-NELSON
Personal Communication Plan: Hitchings and Spence (1991) NFER-NELSON
Pre-Verbal Communication: Kiernan and Reid (1990) NFER-NELSON
Life Experiences Checklist: Ager (1990) NFER-NELSON

Mentally Ill
Psychiatric Hospital Social History Formats
Personality Disturbance: Bedford et al. (1976)
Mental Health: A Client Support Resource Pack: Sutton and Herbert (1992) NFER-NELSON
Health Psychology: Wright et al. NFER-NELSON
Comprehensive Drinker Profile: Miller and Marlatt NFER-NELSON
Inventory of Drinking Situations: Annis NFER-NELSON
Situational Confidence: Annis NFER-NELSON

Physical Disability
Functional Performance Record: Mulhall (1989) NFER-NELSON
Sheffield Screening Test for Acquired Language Disorders: Syder NFER-NELSON (not yet published)
Agency Day Care Criteria

continued

Table 2.3 *continued*

Elderly
Assessment for Residential Care: Neill (1989)
Elderly At Risk in the Community: Taylor (1980)
Goal Planning with Elderly People: Barrowclough and
  Fleming (1986)
Agency Home Help Schedules

Confused Elderly
Guidelines for Social Workers: Gray and Isaacs (1979)
Holden Communication Scale: Holden and Woods (1982)
Clifton Assessment Procedures for the Elderly (CAPE):
  Pattie and Gilleard (1982)
Physical and Mental Impairment of Function Evaluation
  (Pamie): Gurel et al. (1972)
Physical Self-Maintenance Scale (PSMS): Lawton and
  Brody (1969)

* Access to items marked NFER-NELSON is described below.
Other items are in the Bibliography.
  NFER-NELSON operates a scheme whereby social workers
(and other professionals) can register their qualifications and
thereby gain access to appropriate items from the catalogue of
assessment materials which they publish or distribute. For further
information, contact:

NFER-NELSON Publishing Co. Ltd
Darville House
2 Oxford Road East
WINDSOR SL4 1DF
Berkshire
England

Tel: 0753 858600

coherent fashion. The next stage is to make some sense of this
behaviour. Some concepts are needed which will link together
important aspects of this situation. A working model needs to

be developed as to why the situation or behaviour is the way it is. The situation needs to be understood so that decisions can be made and action taken for change. It is at this stage that we need to draw upon a wide range of theoretical material. We must clarify the distinction between 'Practice Theory' and 'Theory for Practice'. Practice Theory is the 'how to' of the process of social work helping. Aspects of Practice Theory are discussed in each section of this book, when we talk about the skills of the worker in relation to the client. (See also Shulman, 1992; Egan, 1975; Lishman, 1991; Coulshed, 1991.)

Theory for Practice, on the other hand, is knowledge drawn from other disciplines and utilised by the social worker. In order to understand how the client relates to the world, we draw on theories based on observation of how people relate to the world. Some of the concepts which can be useful in this phase are listed in Table 2.4.

Once you start to identify significant behaviour, you are venturing into the field of 'norms'. You are likely to be commenting on how appropriate the behaviour is in the particular situations in which you have observed it. It is then important to be clear about the norms by which you are measuring the behaviour. Are you comparing the behaviour with that of an 'average person'? Are you utilising your understanding of the behaviour of someone else of that age, sex, social situation, etc? Are you comparing it with the norm for behaviour with that of others who have a similar ability level in some other sphere?

Behavioural norms do not define right and wrong behaviour. Each of us acts in accordance with certain norms, and contrary to certain other norms. Our individuality includes the ways in which we accord with or depart from norms of behaviour. We use norms to compare one thing with another to give a clearer picture of what we are looking at.

The worker's task is to select from the theories available those which will help in understanding the situation. The theory will be used to understand factors in the client's personality, previous history, and present situation. The selection of theory is influenced by such concepts as loss, change, conflict and role, as illustrated in the examples.

Table 2.4   Some theories for practice

Section A   *Biological and health sciences*
Human development: ages, stages, and the life cycle
Physical needs of the client
Verbal and non-verbal communication theory
Physical illness and its effects
Psychiatric illness and its effects

Section B   *Psychology and sociology*
Maslow and other theories of human needs
Childhood influences on current behaviour (e.g. Freud)
Situations which reinforce particular behaviour (e.g. behaviour theory)
Social and emotional aspects of handicap, loss, illness and mental illness
Family, group and cultural influences on the individual
Effects of institutional life, admission and discharge

Section C   *Organisational theory and social policy*
Legislation pertinent to the client
Function, structures and procedures of your agency and other agencies
Theories of organisations and how they operate
Welfare benefits

2.8   Strengths and needs

At this point in the assessment the material which you and the client have before you needs to be narrowed down, to draw out a list of strengths, limitations and needs. The needs or difficulties will become areas for change. The strengths are

Examples: Use of theory

Child development

Laura, aged 3 years 8 months, attending a family centre
The process of socialisation begins early on at home. Her demands for attention, her continuing need to suck on a dummy, and her inability to eat with a knife and fork are all habits perhaps caused by lack of consistent handling by her mother. Wearing a nappy at night is easier to understand as, having to go outside to a yard toilet where there are often rats about, is daunting to a mother and small child.

Adolescence and learning disability

Paddy O'D, aged 21, attending a day centre
'Adolescence' refers to the psychological changes consequent upon puberty. Its start is fixed by our biological clocks at the beginning of puberty and it ends between age 20 and 25.

Paddy is, I contend, 'adolescing'. This stage of his life is marked by normal developmental stages, and his unique reaction to these.

Paddy is dealing with separation from his parents and having to establish himself in a hostel. His behaviour oscillates between childlike and adult. He sucks his thumb, holds his penis, yet he engages in a creative hobby, recognises and names fractions and decimal points, has shown himself to be a willing and responsible worker, finds it hard to accept criticism, is kind hearted and sensitive, stubborn and unco-operative.

Physical disability and psychology

Robert, aged 52, receiving care at home
As Robert is severely handicapped, the isolated location appears to be unsuitable. However, on looking at the 'whole man' we realise that he is a person who enjoys the peace and beauty of the countryside so in this respect the location is ideal. Robert is sometimes bored and frustrated. Considering that he is a relatively young man and until his accident (which involved a traumatic loss) he had led an active and varied life, this is to be expected.

resources which may be drawn upon in implementing the work. The limitations are potential obstacles to the work. This stage comes immediately before making an explicit agreement with the client about the objectives of work, and before making an explicit recommendation for action within the agency.

The needs of the client must be clearly identified at this stage. The needs could be stated in a table with some brief explanation of key aspects. You will also need some way of recording which issues are important to the client. For example you might put the client's priorities near the top of the list. Also, there may be legal issues which also become priorities.

It is important to summarise strengths as well as major needs. For example many a parent of a handicapped child has been discouraged by the negative tone of the assessment which has been undertaken on their child. A view which includes strengths as well as areas for growth helps the client and family to feel positive about the prospects. It tends to build self-confidence and helps the client to feel good about the work. You need to consider such areas as abilities, feelings, attitudes, circumstances, services available and opportunities, particularly as they relate to the identified needs.

Our perspective on strengths and needs relates both to the client himself and the immediate circumstances, and also to factors further afield. For example, resources in a particular situation may be drawn from:

1 family
2 friends and neighbours
3 informal organisations, such as churches and clubs
4 formal organisations, such as educational institutions, libraries and advisory bodies.

In keeping with our comments about client motivation, it is important that needs are expressed positively. This does not mean ignoring the real issues. Rather, it means expressing the needs in terms of what is desired, rather than purely in terms of what is lacking. This can be much more encouraging. Objectives and resolutions for the coming year are more helpful than listing the things that I was unable to do last year!

Having identified major strengths, limitations and needs, you are ready to begin formulating a plan of action.

Example: Strengths, limitations and needs

Stephen, aged 50, living in a hostel

	Stephen's perception	Worker's perception
Strengths	Good at attending to his own personal care. Good at helping in the kitchen. Likes meeting friends for a drink.	Has good personal hygiene and needs little assistance. Is helpful to care staff. Enjoys getting out and about.
Limitations	Has epilepsy. On tablets.	Suffers from epilepsy. Difficulty managing finances. Poor memory.
Needs	To be alone if he wishes to be. To be able to visit his mother. To be able to stay in the hostel.	Needs personal space. Monitoring medication. Monitoring his state of mind.

---

3 Care planning

3.1 Contracting

In the assessment phase, information about the client has been recorded and classified in some way. This information has been analysed in the light of your knowledge, values, and theoretical material. This full assessment will contain information about the client, together with your judgment of the significant factors relating to the client's personality, previous history and current circumstances. This information has been related to the client's needs or areas for learning as well as to agency aspects such as implications of law and policy.

In the next phase, a plan of care is developed with the client. The assessment ensures that the care is fitted to the client's needs, and also that strengths in the client and his environment are drawn upon. Now you move on to an agreed plan of action so as to change that situation. These two phases of the process are illustrated in Figure 3.1.

It seems most helpful to consider the elements of care planning in three clusters: client issues, worker issues, and agency issues as illustrated in Figure 3.2. All three parts need to be considered concurrently, and in no sense is any one of these three aspects prior to or subsequent to any others.

The starting point is the client and his desire to change. This drive to change behaviour or circumstances may come from a

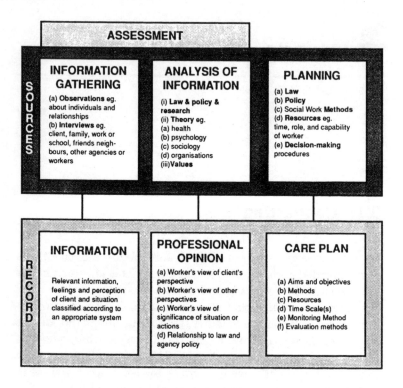

Figure 3.1   The main elements of assessment and planning

variety of sources. Different theorists propose different ways of conceptualising the drive within people.

On the basis of his research, Abraham Maslow arranged human needs in related groups, which he then put in sequence (normally shown as a pyramid as illustrated in Figure 3.3). He proposed that human beings first seek to satisfy their 'lowest level' needs which are physical: food, shelter, clothing and sleep. It is only after these needs are met that the human being

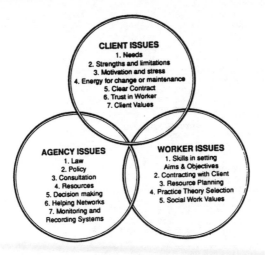

CLIENT ISSUES
1. Needs
2. Strengths and limitations
3. Motivation and stress
4. Energy for change or maintenance
5. Clear Contract
6. Trust in Worker
7. Client Values

AGENCY ISSUES
1. Law
2. Policy
3. Consultation
4. Resources
5. Decision making
6. Helping Networks
7. Monitoring and Recording Systems

WORKER ISSUES
1. Skills in setting Aims & Objectives
2. Contracting with Client
3. Resource Planning
4. Practice Theory Selection
5. Social Work Values

Figure 3.2 Client, worker and agency issues in the care planning phase

will seek to satisfy the second level of needs, which are for security. The needs of clients could be viewed within such a framework (Maslow, 1943, 1970).

A second perspective comes from crisis intervention theories. Their basic tenet is that human beings, like any biological organism, strive to maintain a state of equilibrium, also called 'homeo-stasis'. When the equilibrium is upset, the person enters a period of 'crisis'. Such a period of crisis may be more or less severe depending on a number of factors within the person or the environment, such as his perception of the event, his coping mechanisms, and support from family or neighbours. The worker's role is in harnessing these energies towards resolving the difficulty. The intensity of energy available is very high for a short period of time and it is important to use that energy at the appropriate moment.

A third perspective on client motivation to change is given by the task-centred casework method of social work mentioned in Chapter 1. One aspect of this approach is to give priority to the client's sense of urgency wherever possible, since attempts to impose an agenda for change are rarely successful. The client will apply his greatest energies where he *sees* the need for change.

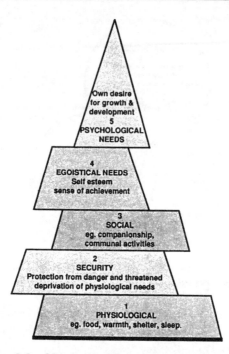

Figure 3.3   Maslow's Hierarchy of Needs

Although we have mostly focused on energies for change, there are also situations where they must be harnessed primarily to prevent deterioration. For example, the care of a dying person in day care at a hospice may require a programme to conserve energies for the performance of daily living tasks (such as dressing) for as long as possible.

We have spoken about the reasons why the client may be seeking help and we must now go on to consider the tentativeness with which the client is likely to be coming to find help. There may be some painful past experiences of social workers. He may have stereotypes about the sort of responses you as an 'authority figure' may give, however ridiculous these may seem to you. The client may be quite resistant to receiving help because of concerns about your competence as a worker. Such feelings are normally called 'ambivalence' in the social work literature. This concept of ambivalence expresses the

Example: Client priority

Andrew, aged 22, attending a day centre
Through the assessment, Andrew, his parents and I agreed on a number of learning needs, including self-care, money management and reading skills. However attitudes to these needs varied considerably. Both Andrew and his parents would support efforts to develop money or reading skills, although Andrew had objections to reading classes perhaps because of an unhappy earlier experience.

After I had explained that from the point of view of the agency any of these three were valid areas for work, we agreed to focus particular attention on money related skills for the next six months.

uncertainty of the person seeking help despite his impetus to change.

It is important for the worker to be aware of both strands of feelings. Do not shy away from talking about the real issues; the client wants solid, real help. On the other hand, the help you are willing to offer may not be received as openly as you would like. It will probably be necessary at some stage to raise the possibility of some of these blockages to the work and you will only be able to do this successfully if you are aware of, and therefore not overcome by, your own feelings.

The concept of ambivalence helps us understand why the 'hidden agenda' of the worker is rarely successful, and is normally unhelpful. If the client does not know what you are about, he is not likely to put his energies into achieving what you have in mind.

An important part of contracting, therefore, is to talk openly, and yet sensitively, about the purpose of the time together and the role of the worker. Although we are discussing the contracting phase at this point, it is clear that these skills and

---

Example: Client ambivalence

Bernie, aged 18, attending an after-care group at an adolescent hostel
Along with other girls who have spent many years in care, Bernie has been attending a series of weekly group sessions to assist in preparing for being mothers one day, since they have little experience of normal family life from which to learn.

After the third session I arranged to see Bernie on her own, explaining that I was concerned by her quietness during the sessions, particularly the last session. Having known something of her in earlier years it seemed uncharacteristic. I asked her if she had been feeling under pressure because of the subject matter i.e. talking about families when she had no contact with her own family.

Bernie at first said that she was happier with the active (pencil and paper) parts rather than just talking. Gradually however, she was able to talk about her own ability to cope with the demands of having children.

After a lengthy session, including some tears, Bernie left reassured that she had not inherited any medical condition from her mother that might predispose her towards suicide, and encouraged that the group was there precisely to support her through such painful feelings.

---

considerations also apply in beginning the assessment. In effect you have to contract to undertake the assessment and it must be clear to the client that your information gathering has been for his sake, not for yours. It is essential that the client be engaged throughout the assessment process and can see the purpose of it. It is helpful to view the assessment as an exploration of the problems with the client. It is unhelpful simply to soak in the answers to the questions without response.

Sometimes new helpers are reluctant to discuss the purpose

Example: Verbal contracting

Miss Cooper, aged 72, temporarily in a residential home

S.W.: I began by saying, 'The last time we met, Miss Cooper, we discussed briefly your changing needs in recent times. I know it can't be easy for you having to leave your home to come into a "group" home and also being uncertain about your future care. If you're feeling down or mixed up about what's going on in your life and you need someone to talk to about it, I am willing to listen. If you're feeling unsure about the future I might be able to help you sort out some of these things or find someone who can, like your friend Mrs Crossley for example. (pause) How are you feeling about these things now, Miss Cooper?'

Miss C.: Oh, I wish I had things sorted out.

S.W.: Yes, there's quite a lot to think about isn't there?

Miss C.: Yes, I could do with your help. I mean, what happens if things aren't sorted out in three weeks? That's all the time I have left here.

---

of their work because of their own embarrassment in discussing the client's problem area. Others may be reluctant because they think they need to 'build a relationship first' before getting on to the real work. Although we recognise that some issues might be better left for discussion after dealing with less threatening matters, our basic premise is that the relationship between the helper and the helped is built *by* working together. This is the purpose of their coming together, and it is this which gives meaning to their relationship. An artificial attempt to 'build a relationship' outside this can leave both worker and client unsure of their purpose in meeting.

In social work the term 'contracting' is often used. Its meaning here is the same as in other spheres of life, although financial

---

Example: A written agreement for work

I have to be ready in time
for bus and to get hand wash up
for tea. I have to be in time dinners and
not to kept Bertie waiting in the
morning and not to kept Bertie waiting
at home time gave me 3 minutes to get
ready in time.

M icheal Brown

We promise to give M.
a 3 minute warning
before each break to
help him be on time.

Ann
Field

---

considerations need not feature at all. It is an agreement, written
or verbal, between different parties about some agreed action
which will be taken either together or by one party on behalf of
the other. It is a mutual understanding about a course of action
designed to achieve specified results. It is an attempt to clarify
the expectations of two or more parties so that they can expect
certain things of each other and clarify their own expectations
over a period of time. Such an agreement takes account of the
aims, needs, resources and skills of each party.

In seeking to have an open honest agreement with a client,
one central skill is to be able to explain clearly the purpose of the
work and the possible ways in which you might be able to help
the client.

Important elements in contracting with clients are shown in

Example: Avoiding jargon

Diane, aged 17, living in a children's home
Diane has been visiting her stepfather Mr McDonald for some months. The relationship has developed well in many respects, but Diane and Mr McDonald have acknowledged some difficulties. They have agreed to my helping them to develop their relationship. Objectives to guide our work were developed together at the start:

Version arising from agency discussions	*Version arising from discussion with Mr McDonald and Diane*
1 To be able to converse beyond a superficial level	1 To be able to talk about things that really matter
2 Mr McDonald's knowledge of adolescent girls and their needs will have improved	2 Mr McDonald will begin to understand the problems Diane is facing in her teenage years
3 Diane's self esteem will improve	3 Diane will begin to like herself more and realise that she is good at doing many things
4 Diane and her stepfather will discuss possible areas of disagreement in order to minimise rows in the family	4 Diane and her stepfather will talk about what they expect of each other

Figure 1.3 under Assessment and Care Planning. Key features are:

1 to clarify with the client the purpose of the work;

2   to clarify with the client your role in this work;
3   to seek honest comment from the client about any proposals
    you make.

For further material on interactional skills in contracting see
Shulman (1992).

3.2   Aims and objectives

We turn our attention now to your contribution as a worker in
this phase of the helping process. Although we have emphas-
ised the priority of the client's sense of urgency in the previous
section this does not in any way make you redundant. Although
another basic principle of our work is to encourage client self-
help and self-determination, the very fact that the client is with
you seeking help indicates that you have something to
contribute. This may only be helping to identify the direction
the work should take, but it is far more likely that the client will
want your help during the process. The translation of 'needs'
into 'aims' should take account of the strengths and limitations
of the client and the situation, something which is often harder
for the person receiving help to see. You are offering your
knowledge and skills to the client to use.
   A key skill the worker can offer in this phase is in selecting
objectives which are both desirable and attainable. It is
discouraging to the client if objectives are agreed which are not
readily achievable, so they need to be planned to leave the client
with a sense of success as an encouragement to go on to the next
stage.

What are aims and objectives?
A dictionary definition is:

AIM: direct at; point out; direct one's ambition;
                purpose.
OBJECTIVE: the point to which the operations are directed;
                the point to be reached; goal.

We will be using 'aim' to describe the general direction of the worker's and client's energies. 'Objective' will be used to describe achievable goals.

Example: Achievability

1 The aim was to engage the whole family.
2 The objective was to enable each family member to address the others at least once during the session.
Number 1 is not an objective as it conveys an intent but no achievable goal.

Example: Whose action?

Consider this statement by a social worker:
'I am here to talk about the causes of depressive feelings'.

Is this something for the worker to achieve, or the client? It says nothing about what the client is expected to achieve from the encounter.

An objective is not only achievable, it is also a description of a proposed change for the person who is learning, growing or being helped. To be able to measure the effectiveness of a programme, the objective must identify attributes or behaviours observable in the person at the end of the process.

How many aims and objectives should I have?
The research on task-centred methods indicated that no more

Example: Behavioural outcomes

Which of these statements comes closest to describing outcomes which can be measured?

1 Trainees will be able to talk about tensions at home.
2 Trainees will have an appreciation of causes of tension at home.
3 Trainees will be able to identify one cause of stress in their own family relationships, with reference to their own behaviour in particular situations.

Number 1 describes what happens in the counselling sessions, but does not indicate outcomes. (It might be an initial objective.) Number 3 is most specific.

---

than three problem areas (aims) should be tackled in any one period of intervention. However you may have a series of objectives related to the achievement of each aim.

Can we tackle more than one area at a time?
Part of your contribution as a professional helper is to assist the client to set *realistic* and *achievable* objectives. If the client's energies are too diversified, little will be achieved. However you may have work on two aspects consecutively or concurrently.

In general the worker is seeking at this stage to encourage constructive and rational thinking by the client about the problems. Some clients need help to overcome thought patterns which are illogical, superstitious or fatalistic. The worker can help the client to consider the range of possible strategies and encourage positive thinking towards a resolution of difficulties.

Another contribution of the worker is to assist in the setting of realistic time limits to different parts of the work. In general, short-term work harnesses client energies better than long-term work. In this context 'short-term' means up to about three

---

Example: Aim and objectives

Aim 1　　　　For Mrs McEvoy to develop her social network by use of the telephone. (Initial Assessment level: Mrs McEvoy knew how to dial.)

Objective 1　To identify a friend to assist in the project.

Objective 2　To enable Mrs McEvoy to learn to use a pay phone. (These necessary skills would need to be defined.)

Objective 3　To provide materials and assistance for Mrs McEvoy to compile a personal telephone directory.

Example: Consecutive objectives

Mrs Faulkner, aged 50, referral from a casualty department

Objective 1　　　　For Mrs Faulkner to stop making
(approx. 6 weeks)　suicidal gestures by having an opportunity to work through her most acute feelings of loss through bereavements.

Objective 2　　　　For Mrs Faulkner to increase her
(approx. 6 weeks)　social contacts either by applying for a job or by developing family relationships (to be decided after part 1).

---

months. Programmes with clients can be structured as concentrated periods focused on specific objectives for about this period of time (say, two to four months). The sort of energy

Example: Concurrent objectives

Mrs Gillespie, aged 69, receiving care at home

Aim
To resume interests enjoyed when her sister was alive, re-establishing some contacts and outings within her community.

Objectives   **Week**

Objective 1 To be able to talk about her feelings of loss at the death of her sister.		--- 0
	Objective 2 To tackle some practical problems arising from her sister's death – in particular Mrs G. hasn't been out of the house since then.	--- 2
Objective 3 To discuss specific requirement of Objective 4 and to prepare for this if Mrs G. decides to proceed.		--- 4
		--- 6
		--- 8
Objective 4 (The main motivator for Mrs Gillespie) To be able to attend a forthcoming conference in her church.		--- 10
		--- 12

required to cope with a major stress or crisis cannot be sustained much beyond this period without in itself leading to a complicating factor in the individual's capacity to cope. The stress is likely to become observably disabling. Clearly, though, a learning programme may have far less emotional content, and could be sustained over a much longer period of time.

Example: Care plan

Valerie, aged 45, attending a day centre

Aims

1 To enable Valerie to become more independent at home.
2 To provide Valerie with a challenge and some responsi-bility in a social situation where she could develop self-confidence and social skills.

Objectives

1 To help Valerie to learn to use an automatic washing machine. (She has one but cannot use it.)
2 To have the co-operation of her brother when we move from the day centre to home for her teaching. (See 1)
3 To investigate the possibility of a work placement for Valerie at a local nursery school (or another work placement if this is not possible).
4 To set up and monitor a work placement matched to Valerie's developmental needs.
5–10 Other objectives related to liaison, Valerie's skill development, transport, self-presentation for work, evaluation of the plan and Valerie's enjoyment of the experiences.

A second area of skill is in identifying resources to help. Who should be involved, and at what stage in the process? Some helping agencies or people may be known by the worker, but not by the client. The client may need help and encouragement in preparing to seek assistance from some particular person. The worker may have a more objective view than the client of the help available from different sources.

Example: Objectives, methods and resources

Paddy O'D, aged 21, attending the day centre
The assessment indicated that Paddy was late on every one of 25 occasions monitored, usually between two and six minutes. This became a priority because of the conflict it created between Paddy and other people.

The programme had three main elements:

1 Support sessions to discuss progress, tackle problems, give encouragement
2 Prompt programme to run in the day centre and the hostel
3 Teaching programme on the concept of time and change.

An extract from the planning for teaching sessions (element 3):

Objective	Method	Resources
To enable Paddy to recognise the cyclical nature of each week.	Games and verbal/ gestural prompts, recognition of week placing names of 14 days in correct order. Matching cards with names of days to those on a calendar.	Card. Felt tips, scissors. Calendar with Paddy's favourite animals i.e. cats. Paddy's knowledge of related vocabulary: yesterday was . . . . tomorrow is . . . .
To show Paddy how a diary can be used to note significant weekly events.	Discussion re: weekly events. Gateway; deadlines for customers picking up tickets; home on Friday; back on Sunday. Enter these into diary and others suggested by Paddy.	A diary for Paddy to keep. Biro. 1 ticket collection date. Info from workshop instructor (customers collect tickets which have been printed at the day centre).

Indeed, your main role in some circumstances may be to plan a package of care provided entirely by informal helpers and voluntary and private establishments.

Example: Resources

Mrs Hamilton, aged 72, resident in a home
1 Mrs H. – for her skills, self knowledge and inner resources.
2 Mrs H's sister, Mrs O'Hagan – for support, etc. but only if Mrs H. permits.
3 Doctor – for advice and to organise the occupational therapist appointment.
4 Occupational therapist – reassessment of condition, advice regarding mobility and possibly the supply of aids.
5 District nurse – for information, advice and skills.
6 Other unit staff – for primary care, personal skills, encouragement, etc.
7 Unit facilities – small cosy sitting-room for privacy during counselling session.
8 Myself – to organise, counsel and be there for her.

A third skill is in identifying the practice theory most useful to you as a helper in the course of the work. Different practice theories have different implications for the way in which the worker and client interact, and the way that the work is perceived by the client.

At this stage we need to consider systems theory. This theory highlights the importance of the different 'systems' within which the client lives, such as family, friends, neighbours, church, clubs, official bodies, and so on. These systems are important as resources to assist in change (or maintenance). They can be used as positive channels through which the social worker acts for the benefit of the client.

Your choice of practice theory will be related to such issues as the client's particular needs, the circumstances in which the work is to take place, the resources available in the agency and within the client and the situation, and your own particular skills. Some theories have clearer criteria for selection than others. For example the task-centred method clearly identifies situations in which it might be appropriate, and situations in which it is unlikely to be. These criteria are based on research on the outcomes of practice.

3.3   Decision making

Our premise is that you are a worker with a particular role, working within an agency with a particular function. The consequences of this are that there are specific legal, policy and resource issues which will relate to your agency and to your job. If you are simply helping a neighbour as an individual, rather than as a professional member of a helping agency, the policy issues become those of your own values and interests, the legal issues become those of any citizen, and the resource issues become simply your own time and energy. As someone working within an agency which has a specific function within society, defined in some formal manner, you are constrained by a much wider range of considerations.

In some fields of work, for example services to elderly people, the legal situation is relatively static. In other fields there is a continuing cutting edge of case law being generated, for example in child care. Whatever your working situation, you need to be clear about:

- the legal basis for your providing services to this client group;
- the aspects of law pertinent to this particular client's situation.

Policies may be defined in a variety of ways. Some policies are made at national or regional level by the Department of Health and Social Services. Statutory Social Services Departments, and voluntary organisations make their own policies. Within these agencies, policies are applied or 'translated' by middle managers, and by particular teams and units. In some cases

---

Example: Legal aspects

Valerie, aged 45, attends a day centre: summary of legal aspects
Our services to Valerie are provided under the Health and Personal Social Services (N.I.) Order 1972 in Part II 4 (a) relating to provision of Health Services designed to promote the Physical and Mental Health of the people of N. Ireland through the prevention, diagnosis and treatment of illness and in 4 (b) relating to the provision of Personal Social Services to promote Social Welfare.

Valerie was registered as Special Care in 1972 in accordance with the Mental Health (N.I.) Order 1961. This act has been replaced by the Mental Health (N.I.) Order 1986 which no longer requires a register to be maintained.

Although Valerie is cared for at home by her brother, he is not her legal guardian and Section 18 of the Mental Health (N.I.) Order 1986 relating to guardianship does *not* apply in her case.

---

policies are clearly defined in writing (for example, procedure for drugs management within residential homes). In other cases there are areas recognised as requiring a clear mandate from managers even though no written policy may exist (for example, typically sex education for people with learning difficulties).

Your particular agency will provide you with a range of resources, together with certain limitations on how those resources can be used. As well as your own time, you are likely to be able to draw upon the following:

- guidance and support of your line manager;
- support and advice from colleagues;
- advice from other members of the agency;
- clerical support;
- access to information from other agencies;

Example: Agency policy

Mrs McKay, aged 49, soon to be discharged from psychiatric hospital
In order to formulate a care plan with Mrs McKay it was necessary to identify clearly the policies of the agency in relation to mental health work.

DHSS level:

Increased provision of care in the community and less in psychiatric hospitals.

Area Board level:

Development of the mental health resource unit to facilitate care in a range of local hostels and private lodgings.

Unit of Management level:

The resource unit as a place to offer care and to develop skills necessary to promote as 'normal' a lifestyle as possible for clients. A system for prioritising types of need, given that demand is greater than resources.

Unit level:

Current structure of programme on offer and general 'house rules'. Identification of possible programme development.

- physical facilities of accommodation, heating, lighting, and so on;
- access to books and journals in a library;
- such things as paper, pens, flip chart pads, telephone, computer . . .

Effective management of resources is becoming an increasingly prominent part of social services provision at the present time. Skills in acquiring and deploying resources are to be prized!

Decision making is a stage at which your line manager will normally be involved as a matter of agency policy:

- to give support to you as the worker;
- to sanction the use of agency resources;
- to assist in the clarification of legal and policy issues;
- to sanction the use of your time on this particular client;
- to relate your concern for this client to broader agency issues, such as the needs of other clients served by the team or unit.

There may also be more complex systems within the agency for decision making in certain situations. For example within a day care facility for people with learning disabilities, reviews might be held which involve the day-care worker, the field social worker, a clinical psychologist, as well as a member of the management team of the day centre. Within a residential home for children, reviews might involve the primary worker within the home, the team leader within the home, the field social worker, the field work team leader, and the external manager responsible for decisions made.

There may be clear policy decisions already in existence on the frequency and format of decision-making meetings about the care of clients. So, although in some situations, decisions might be made simply by consulting with your line manager, in other situations a broader consultation may be desirable or required.

There are clearly significant advantages in having a multi-agency forum for decision making in certain situations. The sharing of information gives each agency a fuller picture of the situation and should enable better founded decisions to be made. Risks can be minimised and responsibilities shared (Brearley, 1982). The efforts of the different workers should be better co-ordinated. The availability of certain resources should be clearer. Finally, work may be allocated more effectively. This may raise issues about the contribution which different agencies make and the confidentiality which can be assured within a particular agency. Allocation of work should be determined primarily by the needs of the client, but there is sometimes a

Example: Home Care planning

Mrs McKillop, aged 80, was in hospital having suffered a major stroke causing right side hemiplegia. The GP referred her to the social worker for respite care. He considered that she could only be cared for in a residential or nursing home. But as Mrs McKillop was adamant that she would not go into a home, and as he needed the bed in the GP unit for another patient, he referred her for respite care in the hope that she would change her mind about long term admission once she was introduced to the home. He did not think that she could be cared for at home both because of her health needs and because of her 'personality', not to mention six cats that seemed to dictate the hygiene standards!

The social worker visited the client and the Ward Sister, and at this screening stage decided that an occupational therapist and district nurse should be involved in a fuller assessment. She also ascertained that the client was adamant about returning to her own home. Relatives were contacted, but they did not want to have anything to do with providing care for her at home.

The social worker and occupational therapist undertook a joint assessment visit to the client in hospital and to the client's home (with the client's consent). They found that Mrs McKillop could walk short distances using a walking aid and with staff assistance. She was continent with regular toileting, but required help with this. The district nurse visited subsequently regarding the need for a commode and any other cover from a nursing point of view that might be required.

Having had some initial thoughts about a possible home care package, the social worker visited the GP and gained reluctant consent to attempting care at home.

continued

Home Care planning *continued*

Mrs McKillop agreed to a period of respite care in a residential home so that a clearer assessment of her abilities could be made. Just before discharge from hospital, one relative (a nephew) agreed to assist with certain aspects of home care. At this stage application for Attendance Allowance was made. Within the home, the residential staff gave encouragement and opportunity for Mrs McKillop to develop skills so as to be as independent as possible, and to recognise her own limitations. This also began to build up a possible contingency arrangement in case of an emergency.

The social worker sought formal agreement from the senior social worker (team leader) to a Home Care plan whilst the other professionals agreed their inputs with their own line management.

Initial action to implement Home Care

- Occupational therapist arranged for rail outside front door, raised toilet seat, a lock on the door to upstairs (following Mrs McKillop's agreement to sleep down-stairs), removal of door saddles and advice on the purchase of a new bed.
- Nephew bought a new bed.
- District nurse provided commode.
- ACE (Action for Community Employment) workers redecorated house, checked fire, cleaned chimney, etc.

Daily care (HCA means Home Care Assistant)

8.00 am–9.00 am   HCA lights fire, assists out of bed, helps with personal washing, gives medication, provides breakfast, empties commode, makes bed; also disposes of incontinence pads or changes sheets if necessary.

continued

Home Care planning *continued*

11.30 am–11.45 am	HCA walks Mrs McKillop (exercise) to toilet, refuels fire, leaves out medication.
12 noon	Lunch from Residential Home (client pays). Mon–Fri delivered by ACE worker (client pays). Sat–Sun delivered by HCA run.
2.00 pm–2.30 pm	HCA makes cup of tea, washes up lunch dishes, refuels fire, assists to toilet, tidies, washes kitchen floor, etc.
5.00 pm–5.30 pm	HCA prepares and serves evening meal, refuels fires, assists to toilet, washes dishes. Mrs McKillop encouraged to help plan meals.
8.00 pm–8.45 pm	HCA prepares and serves supper, assists to toilet, gives medication, assists to bed, attends to home safety, ensures telephone and torch working and accessible.
11.00 pm–11.15 pm	HCA check-up visit.

1 hour per week HCA doing washing and ironing in own home.

Once per week: District nurse provides bed-bath, cuts finger-nails and other nursing duties as necessary.

Home Care funding: 16 hours social services budget, 7 hours Attendance Allowance (state benefit) per week.

Regular care

HCA: washes hair as necessary.
Chiropodist cuts toe-nails as necessary.

continued

Home Care planning *continued*

Nephew oversees financial affairs including paying bills and collecting benefits. He lived close by and agreed to visit daily, even if only briefly.
Monitoring of general care by social worker; (calls on O.T. as necessary).
GP visits occasionally and monitors medical condition through district nurse.

Emergency planning

Client can telephone nephew or Home Care Assistant.
Keys kept by: Home Care Assistant, nephew, social services.
Relief Home Carers identified.
Residential home as final resort for emergencies.

Note: Mrs McKillop returned home after 8 months in hospital and 1 month in residential care. She is content living at home a year later.

---

requirement for other agencies to be involved in certain decisions.

Whether the client should be present at a formal large-scale decision-making meeting is normally a matter for agency policy rather than a decision to be made by an individual worker. Normally there are clear advantages in involving the client, but there can be overriding disadvantages. The basic principle is to seek client consent and full participation unless there is a justifiable reason not to do so.

Whether the client's family should be involved at a decision-making meeting raises similar questions. It is in any case important that the effect of any decision on other family members be considered.

We have focused here on the formal decision-making system. However you will be aware also of the informal systems of

---

Example: Client involvement in decision making

Lisa, aged 40, attending a day centre
One aim of the work was to promote client choice and independence. In order to do this most effectively, it was planned that her new symbolic care plan should be integrated into the existing system of six-monthly reviews. Clients are often overawed by 'the review' and reluctant to speak out. The worker held a pre-review meeting with Lisa. They talked about the daily activities in the unit, those she liked to do and what changes she would like to make. Lisa was encouraged to speak out for herself and told about the purpose and format of the review.

During her review, Lisa appeared more at ease than on previous occasions. She spoke out more confidently and said what she wanted to do. She occasionally needed a prompt from the notes of the pre-review meeting.

A programme of care was then agreed on to include her needs and wishes. The next day the worker met Lisa and her written care plan was put into symbolic form using the system which had been developed with Lisa and her group over the past 3 months. She was most enthusiastic and confidently 'read' her daily activities with ease.

---

influence both within and outside organisations. The support of the staff team within the unit is crucial to real success with a client programme. Hence, although only certain members may be present at the formal decision-making meeting, it is important to consider communication with other members of your team.

From this decision-making process, there should come a coherent and comprehensive care plan including at least the following elements:

- aims and objectives;

Example: Family implications

An assessment on 50-year-old Martin attending a day centre revealed that he had little ability to peel vegetables, although he seemed physically able to do so. A broader assessment of Martin's social situation showed that he lived with his sister who also had a learning disability. Between them they had worked out, over many years, arrangements for running their household. In this case Susan normally prepared meals, whilst Martin looked after the fires, and they each went shopping on alternate days. Clearly a meaningful day-centre programme (for example, to help Martin to cope when his sister went into hospital occasionally) needed to be worked out with full regard to his normal lifestyle.

- methods and roles;
- time-scale;
- resources;
- monitoring methods;
- review date.

The proposed care or counselling is then put into effect. This stage of the process is illustrated in Figure 3.4.

3.4 Planning: an overview

The three main aspects of social work – client, worker and agency need to be considered in parallel and held in balance at all stages of the social work process. This is shown in diagram form in Figure 3.5, with an explanation and example of each given in Table 3.1.

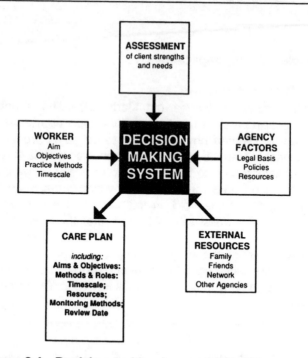

Figure 3.4   Decision making in care planning

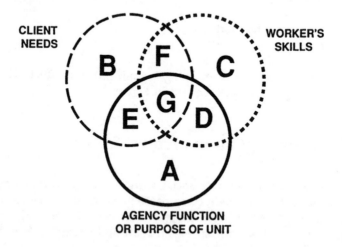

Figure 3.5   To illustrate the common ground of client, workers and agency aspects in care planning

Table 3.1 Explanation and examples of Figure 3.1

	Section of diagram	Example: Assessment of needs of an elderly person living alone
A	Agency or unit services not relevant to this client group	Child care services
B	Client needs not met by this agency	Interest in oil painting, meals-on-wheels
C	Worker skills not relevant to this client or agency work	Cycling
D	Worker skills appropriate to job but not to this client	Organising respite care
E	Client needs met by another worker in the agency	Referral to occupational therapist re: need for a handrail on the stairs
F	Worker's personal skills which might help client but not part of the job	Interest in water colour painting
G	The focus of the agreed work with the client, where the client's needs, the worker's skills and the agency function coincide	Management of home help service; grant for telephone installation; assist in reorganising living arrangements; loss counselling

4 Implementation

4.1 Being helped

Although this chapter is on the implementation of the helping process, it must be borne in mind that many of the skills mentioned may also be used in other phases of the work (for example empathic skills during the assessment and contracting phases). Conversely, some of the skills described in previous chapters may also be used in the implementation phase (for example, contracting is required on a sessional basis, not only on a one-off occasion).

Our major focus in this chapter is on the actions you are going to take to help your client. Before considering these, however, it is worthwhile to look at the situation from the client's perspective. In Chapter 2 we discussed tuning-in, that is attempting to understand the client's view of his situation. But what is the client looking for from you, the helper? If you have received help from another person, the experience should certainly help you to understand the qualities the person being helped is looking for. Perhaps such things as:

Empathy	Warmth	Genuineness
Encouragement	Caring	Reliability
Respect	Helpfulness	Promptness
Clarity	Concern	Effectiveness
Competence	Trustworthiness	Confidentiality

You cannot create such qualities overnight in yourself if you do not already possess them. However some thoughtfulness about the needs of the client can make a vast difference to the ability and effectiveness of the help offered.

Another aspect of the client perspective is to consider what it is that makes a good client! Some of us are more able than others to make use of help from another person. Some useful characteristics might be:

willingness to look at the problems;
ability to understand the situation;
commitment to an appropriate course of action.

4.2   Strategies for action

Some situations require minimal assistance. For example, someone may wish for help in writing a letter, or may be seeking information which you can provide. This may occur in any setting, to a fieldworker on office duty or visiting a client in his own home, to a residential or day-care worker in an unplanned contact with a resident or member. In such situations only a minimal use of the model we have described is made, although most parts of it will be applicable in principle. You are likely to make a decision yourself about the response to give (planning phase). An important consideration in such situations is the extent to which the worker takes control in the situation and the extent to which the client is empowered to take action. This is illustrated by the spectrum of responses shown in Figure 4.1.

Many responses to clients by social workers fall into the category of minimal intervention, but there is always the risk that a major need will be missed. The worker must undertake the assessment in sufficient detail to make a professional decision as to the need for deeper work.

In general, the worker is seeking to support client initiatives and control of the work, to utilise informal caring networks and

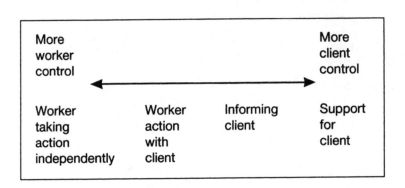

Figure 4.1 Spectrum of control in intervention

volunteers, and only to initiate planned in-depth help from a major agency when necessary (Taylor, 1989).

4.3 Approaches to helping

Broadly speaking we identify five major strands to social work:

1 Counselling with individuals, couples and families.
2 Mediation.
3 The provision of physical care.
4 Developmental methods.
5 Social groupwork.

We have taken the view that residential institutions, day care, and hospitals are settings within which social work takes place, rather than seeing these as methods of social work in themselves. Most social work methods are applicable to work with most client groups in most settings.

Counselling
We have provided a very brief note on some major theories and have attempted to divide them into five types shown in Figure 4.2 as an aid to selecting practice theory. Brief notes on practice

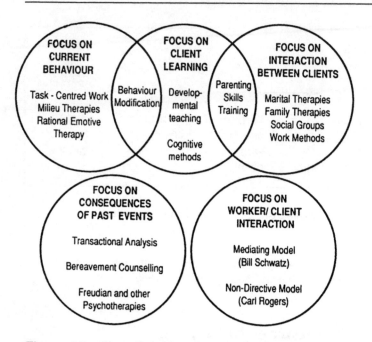

**Figure 4.2   Grouping of major approaches to helping
individuals**

theory are given in Table 4.1. For further information on
individual theories see Shulman (1992), Egan (1975), Lishman
(1991) and other key texts.

Mediation
Part of the social work role involves mediation or advocacy on
behalf of clients, for example, in some instances where there is
conflict or misunderstanding between a client and an organisation.

Physical care
Physical caring is not confined to residential facilities. Both day
care and fieldwork staff can become involved in providing
physical care. Bathing and hair washing in a day-care setting
may be essential components of the care of an elderly person
living at home. Fieldworkers also may have occasion to 'roll

Table 4.1 Brief notes on practice theories

1 *Task Centred Work*
   Utilises achievable, agreed goals over an agreed time-span to achieve change desired by the client.

2 *Milieu Therapy*
   Utilises the environment in which the client is placed as a means of facilitating change.

3 *Rational Emotive Therapy* (Ellis)
   Counselling based on the premise that our feelings in a situation will depend on our beliefs and perceptions of events.

4 *Behaviour Modification*
   Utilises specific, planned rewards as a means of promoting the desired behaviour.

5 *Developmental Teaching*
   Uses programmes to continue natural progression of knowledge and skills utilising assessment of developmental needs.

6 *Cognitive Methods*
   Utilises agreed strategies for learning knowledge and skills that will enhance problem solving on living skills.

7 *Parenting Skills Training*
   May use a variety of approaches (e.g. behavioural, group reinforcement) to develop skills in child rearing.

8 *Marital Therapies*
   Again a range of approaches (e.g. interactionist, behavioural) applied to marital situations.

9 *Family Therapies*
   A wide range of approaches (e.g. structural, systemic, role sculpting) utilising the family as focus rather than individual.

10 *Mediating Model* (Schwartz)
   Utilises detailed analysis of helping skills and views worker as mediating between client and other parties (Shulman, 1992).

continued

Table 4.1 *continued*

11 *Non-Directive Counselling* (Rogers)
    Utilises detailed analysis of helpful qualities (empathy, warmth, genuineness) in counselling relationship.

12 *Transactional Analysis*
    Looks at current behaviour in terms of 'Parent', 'Adult' and 'Child' inner 'scripts' and early influences on this (Pitman, 1984).

13 *Psycho-Dynamic Model* (Freud)
    Looks at behaviour in terms of 'ego', 'superego' or 'id' and psycho-sexual childhood development.

their sleeves up and get stuck in' to complement the more usual system of care by home helps. Providing care in a way which respects the dignity and wishes of the recipient is part of social work practice.

Developmental methods

The task of facilitating learning and growth for clients (for example those with learning disability attending day care) means that social workers often have to draw on a range of theories of development and approaches to child and adult learning. Some examples are cognitive approaches which have similarities with social work methods such as the task-centred casework method, and behavioural learning approaches akin to behavioural methods in individual counselling.

Social groupwork

Many creative developments are taking place in residential and day-care settings in terms of groupwork. For example reminiscence, reality orientation and activity groups in homes for elderly people; groups concerned with foster preparation or leaving care in children's homes; groups for specific client groups in day care, such as those recently disabled, as well as the conventional activity, educational or occupational programme (Benson, 1987; Shulman, 1992).

Our focus here is on the care of individuals, ie. the framework and process that underpins particular types of social work service such as counselling, mediation, physical care and developmental work with individuals.

4.4 Monitoring and recording

Monitoring is an essential component in ensuring that the quality of the service provided meets the standard which you have set in your agency. Some of the quality standards are requirements from outside the agency. It is useful to look at monitoring and recording from the perspective of the people or purposes which it serves. The list in Table 4.2 is a summary of major reasons why clients, workers, colleagues in other agencies, management, and the law, might require monitoring and recording. Your system for monitoring the progress of the work will be influenced by the records you have to keep, which should cover the major aspects you might in any case wish to monitor.

The professional worker with the best knowledge of the client is normally the best person to complete the first report or record. Another consideration is the authority to disseminate the report and whether it should be countersigned by another party. For example, a court report from a children's home might be written by the child's primary worker and countersigned by the head of unit, which gives added authority to what is written.

A good record or report should be:

- clear
- concise
- accurate
- objective
- relevant

- factual – distinguishing between:
  (a) matters directly observed
  (b) matters reported by others, identifying sources
  (c) opinions
  (d) professional assessment

Records and reports are only of use in so far as they are of value to the reader. Retrievability of the information is para-

Table 4.2   Purposes of monitoring and recording

Client	An overall assessment. An understanding of the contract or agreement with the worker. Some way to record success or achievement.
The worker	An aid to your memory of facts. A safeguard in case of allegations. For your learning and development. As a tool to help develop objectivity. For accountability and workload management.
Colleagues	To provide continuity such as transfer of case, handover time, passing of messages, induction of new staff.
Other agencies	Records necessary for effective multi-disciplinary working, ranging from the simple record in a day book, of a resident's illness in a home for the elderly to the more complex agreements required in child abuse situations.
Management	Information for accountability of the worker. Ensuring that the appropriate services are provided effectively and economically. Making decisions about client care and use of resources. Ensuring that policies and procedures are followed.

The law	Records required under:
	
	Dangerous Drug Legislation
	Health & Safety Legislation
	Health & Personal Social Services
	  Legislation
	Employment Legislation
	Client Group Legislation in particular Child Care and Mental Health
	
	For court evidence (e.g. Coroner or
	  Juvenile Court)
	Accountability regarding client's property

Example: Recording: Diary of events

Mark and Mavis attending a family therapy unit within a family and child care team

Numbered — items for cross-referencing

6	Mrs McMullan, H.V.	
Telephone call received 20.4.90	Discussed development of Matthew.	

Clear item — headings

7	Decision taken to offer work in family therapy unit. (see minutes)
Case Conference 23.4.90	
8	Arranged home visit.
Telephone call 24.4.90	

Clear dates —

9	19.30–21.00	— Times, when useful
Home visit 26.4.90	*Mark and Mavis* Invitation to family unit and forming agreement for work. Well received.	

10	16.00–17.30	— Concise summary
Family unit	*'Session 1'* Completing agreement for work (see signed agreement) and observation of interactions with children. (notes to Assessment Report)	

Example: Aide-memoire for assessment report

Observation: Mavis with children
Verbal: clear and concise explanations, low-toned commands, not followed up.
Physical: limited contact at first. More with daughter (she sought more attention).
Play: divided her time between children. They to her rather than she to them.

Future work
Implementation of instructions to children?
Use of positive reinforcement?
Physical contact with son – why so little?

Observations: Mark with children
etc.

'secondary filing system' came into operation. It is permissible to make notes to aid practice and as an aide-memoire about events, but these must be destroyed at regular intervals. The material should be incorporated into a report in the file or disregarded as irrelevant.

It is also possible to include a client's own recording in your file (see the example on pages 82–3).

The ongoing recording of accurate, retrievable information and the summarising of information at intervals (see Chapter 5) are the cornerstones of monitoring the quality of care provision.

excercise but wasn't so good at them on Thursday. On 19th June, Stephen discussed with me a regime of exercise he had laid out for me. I must admit I was apprehensive about starting the exercises as I had a negative approach to everything but Stephen reassured me and put my mind at rest. On 23rd June Stephen assisted by Rachel started the exercises every Monday and Thursday. The majority of exercises were taken from a book written by a physiotherapist and published by MS Society/Action. Any exercises I didn't fully understand Stephen would demonstrate on a person and explain exactly how it was done. On days I wasn't feeling so well I worked lightly on the exercises and worked more enthusiastically on days I was in a better frame of mind. In concluding, this has given me a feeling of well-being and a more positive outlook to life. I must sincerely thank Rachel and Stephen both of whom have been a tower of strength to me during these past few months.

5 Evaluation

5.1 Principles of evaluation

The system of evaluation you use needs to be designed and built in from the start of the work. In identifying your evaluation tools, you might wish to ask the following questions:

1 What is to be evaluated?
2 Why is it being evaluated?
3 Who is to undertake evaluation?
4 How is evaluation to be managed?
5 What indicators of change or progress are going to be used?
6 How is the information gathering to be carried out (through questions, observation, or reading)?
7 How is the comparison with the initial assessment to be carried out?
8 Is the theoretical basis for your evaluation sound?
9 Will the evaluation you have designed be appropriate for possible changes of practice and the other purposes for which it is designed?
10 When will a summary evaluation have to be presented?

In its simplest form an evaluation needs to say:

- What was the problem?
- What action has been taken?

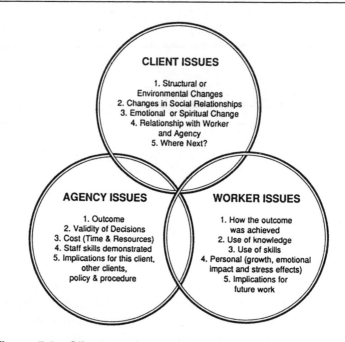

Figure 5.1   Client, worker and agency issues in the evaluation phase

- What is the outcome?
- What use has been made of resources?

Some of the reasons why evaluation should be undertaken are illustrated in Figure 5.1.

Many social work establishments conduct 'reviews' on or with their clients. A review is essentially a combination of an assessment of the current situation and an evaluation of work which has already taken place. Planning future action is also a normal feature of 'reviews'.

The review or evaluation is a summarising of the ongoing evaluation which is in fact a continuing and concurrent part of the work. The client will almost certainly be evaluating the service received at frequent intervals and his investment of time and energy will only continue if the service received is of value. For the worker, corrective feedback at intervals may be very helpful in adjusting the course of the work. For the agency, concurrent recording is normally a required component of professional practice.

Another device is to undertake an 'interim evaluation' perhaps at a mid-way or third-way time through the period of work. The interim evaluation becomes a marker to check that the work is on course.

As in the earlier phases of work, the evaluation and ending phase is carried out by the worker with the client and in conjunction with the agency mandate. The client will certainly have feelings about the progress or otherwise of the work and any reluctance to talk about it is normally more related to the sense of taboo felt by the worker than to a lack of ideas on the part of the client.

Discussion of the worker–client relationship may be an even more difficult subject. Failure to address any difficulties or pains in the helping process may, however, make it more difficult for the client to seek help in future. If there have been painful moments, it is almost always better to raise and discuss these, rather than to leave matters unresolved. Conversely, where a helping relationship has been experienced positively, open (even if brief) discussion of 'how we have worked together' can consolidate the work that has taken place, help to establish where the relationship is, and may give a sense of satisfaction to both parties. Whether or not future work is undertaken by this client with yourself as a worker, it is valuable to raise the issue of where the client is going next, as part of this ending process.

5.2 Measuring effectiveness

The work which has been undertaken has been planned on the basis of a professional assessment. However it is not necessarily a perfect plan. It is basically an optimal plan, that is the best plan in the circumstances (Brearley, 1982). There are risks inherent in any plan, and particularly in plans concerned with human beings. The information available at the start will not be complete and human behaviour is not totally predictable even

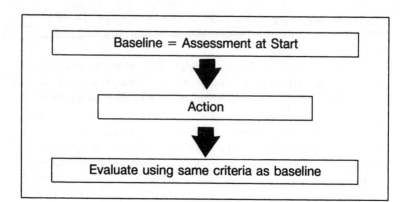

Figure 5.2 Basic principle of evaluation using a baseline

Example: Using a baseline

Paddy O'D, aged 21, attending a day centre
In order to measure the development of Paddy's ability at time-keeping, a baseline was established at the beginning of the programme. The same measuring system was then used at the end of the 6-week programme.

Start:

Mins. late	7	6	5	4	3	2	1	0
No. of times	0	1	1	4	7	7	3	1

i.e. out of 24 opportunities, he was on time once.

End:

Mins. late	7	6	5	4	3	2	1	0
No. of times	0	0	0	1	1	4	2	16

i.e. out of 24 opportunities, he was on time 16 times.

where good information is available. The purpose of evaluation, then, is primarily to compare the outcome with what was planned.

Applying measures of evaluation to personal counselling work can seem cold-blooded. However it is important that we as a profession evaluate our own work, otherwise the work is likely to be undervalued (see Reith, 1988).

The clarity of the aims and objectives agreed at the beginning of the work will have a major bearing on the quality of evaluation which can be undertaken when the work is complete. It is possible and indeed appropriate in some situations to specifically establish a baseline from which to measure progress (see Figure 5.2). This is often used in work with clients with learning difficulties. The same assessment can then be carried out at the completion of the piece of work so that the results before and afterwards can be compared. It is also possible to consider an evaluation after some time has elapsed from the completion of the work. However this is often more difficult to implement (see Sheldon, 1988).

It is clearly easier to undertake thorough evaluation in some situations than others. Where more than one individual is involved, the complexity of human interactions makes the amount of material to be assessed much greater, rendering accurate evaluation more difficult (see Feek, 1988).

Our focus is on joint evaluation between the client and the agency providing the service, in which the worker may act as the representative of the agency. Sometimes the worker evaluates the work through discussions with the client and his supervisor separately; sometimes the evaluation may involve a more senior member of staff as well as the worker and client.

The client may need help from the worker in evaluating the service received. This may seem threatening at first, but is a component of good practice. See example on p. 94.

Social workers should generally strive for a scientific approach to measuring outcomes, including both qualitative and quantitative aspects. How people feel about a situation is important as well as the reality. For example, a resident may comment on 'the improved atmosphere in the sitting-room'. This may be the result of work on joint activities, personal space, or new agreements about communal chores and ways of handling

Example: Evaluating outcomes, planning and process

Mrs Owens, aged 68, a widow, was admitted a year ago to a home for confused elderly people. Mrs Owens suffers from the early stages of senile dementia and her financial affairs are managed by the Office of Care and Protection under Mental Health legislation.

Her background, very briefly, is that her mental impairment commenced when her husband died. For Mrs Owens, this was a multiple loss (Kubler-Ross, 1970):

loss of her husband
loss of her role as a wife
loss of control of her finances
loss of relationship with son due to alcoholism (precipitated by his father's death)
loss of personal esteem as family members began taking over responsibility for her
loss of freedom of movement as family members began to 'granny sit' to keep her safe in her own home
loss of status as a mother when her children began to 'tell her off' for her behaviour, and her son was physically aggressive towards her.

The AIM at this stage of the programme in the residential home was to help Mrs Owens to develop self esteem. Some specific OBJECTIVES were:

(a)   to create a climate conducive to Mrs Owens developing a new role in the home
(b)   to give a personal allowance weekly and facilitate trips to town for personal shopping
(c)   to increase family contact to once per week.

continued

Evaluating outcomes *continued*

Evaluation of outcomes (summary of main points)

(a) *Create a climate conducive to Mrs Owens developing a new role in the home*
   Domestic staff now accept that Mrs Owens plays a regular role in laying the tables for meals. Of her own accord, she has added to the tasks that we provided. She is beginning to diversify, for example by helping our laundress to distribute clean clothing. Humour is evident also: the staff teasingly say to her 'the boss is putting you on our duty sheet' and she roars with laughter.

(b) *Personal allowance and shopping*
   After surmounting the legal and procedural difficulties in achieving this it went smoothly. To Mrs Owens £7 is a lot of money, but she does not understand its present value. When her notes are changed in the shops or restaurants she becomes very confused by the new coinage. However it has given her much satisfaction to have her own money and we intend to continue to do this.
   The trips to town were always on offer, but in the latter weeks of the programme Mrs Owens did not always avail herself of them. She chose instead to be with her craft group or just rest following her 'day's work'.

(c) *Family contact*
   Generally family members are visiting more frequently and are happier that the relationship with their mother has returned to two-way. The son who suffers from alcoholism, for the last three weeks of this programme and to the date of writing this, has been 'dry'. He has said that the death of his father was bad enough but his mother's behaviour 'cut him up' and then he felt guilty about putting her into care and his treatment of her beforehand. This we felt was insightful on his part. He attributes his non-drinking to the improvement in his mother.

continued

Evaluating outcomes *continued*

Evaluation of planning (some key points)
The preparatory groundwork was extensive and initially it was felt that no stone had been left unturned. In practice it was found that whilst the team directly involved with Mrs Owens were well prepared (and felt that they were), the remainder of the unit staff lacked the same depth of preparation. Fortunately this was identified in week 1 of the programme, and corrected over the following week.

A second issue was that whilst the deputy had been asked to ensure that one or more of the primary care team were on duty, this had not always been possible.

Evaluation of process (some key points)
1   The process was smooth and effective. It was sometimes difficult to get the primary care team together for weekly evaluation purposes. This was overcome by the good will of individual team members, who showed commitment beyond 'their call of duty'. During week 1 night staff were antagonistic to the programme because Mrs Owens was very restless for three nights. They accepted that this was a transient phase, as was borne out later. The contribution of domestic and catering staff proved invaluable, producing more cohesion in the workforce and giving to each group a greater understanding of the others' jobs and pressure of work.

The reaction of a care assistant on one of the trips was illuminating. She noticed a reflection of herself and Mrs Owens in a shop window and all of a sudden thought 'I'm the institutionalised one'. She explained that she was aimlessly grabbing for Mrs Owen's arm to 'link on' and she felt naked because Mrs Owens had a handbag and shopping bag whereas she only had a purse. When she related this to other staff, whilst there was teasing, I feel a valuable message was also being received.

2   In discussing our spring in-service training topics, it was interesting to note the number requesting further learning on observation skills and programme planning.

pressure. The work and developments are easier to measure than the feelings, but both are important.

Evaluation is a feedback mechanism, providing a summary and a measure of what has taken place for the planning of the next steps. There may be continuing work on a further or different area, or possibly the end of the work (see Figure 5.3).

5.3 Worker skills

'Where next?' is an essential part of assisting the client to transfer learning and take courage to move forward. This may be particularly true where the worker is ending contact, and where the client is going to proceed with fewer supports in future.

The worker needs to be aware of the feelings of the client connected with endings. Leaving the support of the worker can raise feelings of loss, and the worker needs to be aware of the ways in which they may find expression. The client may not seem to acknowledge that the worker is actually finishing contact. Sadness at losing this worker may express itself as anger. Bargains about meeting up next year or sending holiday postcards may be made. The task of the worker is to recognise and to address these most powerful feelings (Shulman, 1992).

A vital aspect of evaluation is for the worker to evaluate his or her own part in the process. This is sometimes termed 'self-evaluation'. A summary of the outcome of the work itself is not the same thing as describing the part you have played in achieving that outcome. Your own role has included a contribution to assessment, planning and implementation. It is useful to ask questions about your work in each of these phases, both in terms of outcome and in terms of the process or relationship with the client. There are three useful questions to ask:

1 What knowledge has been used?
2 What skills have been used and developed?
3 What has the impact been upon yourself emotionally, in terms of stress, and in personal growth?

Example: Evaluation by a client

When I first knew that I was going to be coming to the family centre I was not pleased about it because I had been before and that time found it was a waste of everyone's energy and time. There were no directions or aims. This time has been a lot different. Being able to talk to someone rather than being talked to has made a big difference. I feel I have got a lot more from this programme. I would now be more inclined to express my opinions or ask questions than before, also it has made me less reactive towards criticism.

The practical help leaflets and reading material etc has been interesting to read but some of the practical skills — bathing, sterilising and bottlemaking — I did wonder about the usefulness of all that as the baby was a month or so old when I came here and I knew what to do, also having other children I had done the bathing and sterilising before. Though I knew that these skills had to be seen, that I was able to do them.

I feel that the aims of the programme have been met, especially the relationship. I always feel at ease coming here and I don't feel that I have to come down. Although I know that I do.

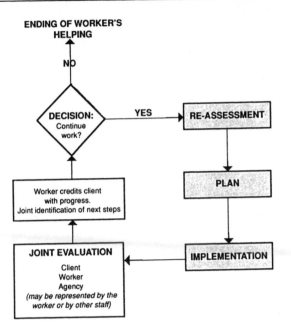

Figure 5.3 Evaluation phase

This part of the evaluation is not part of the client's concern, though you might sometimes wish to share something of your own learning with the client.

6 Managing the work

6.1 Primary worker systems

Assessment and care planning should be undertaken by practitioners who are suitably qualified and in an appropriate role. In this section we address the need for systems to organise and support staff involved in assessing needs and planning care, as well as issues related to the development of new systems for care management.

In residential units, primary worker systems have developed to provide more personalised care than used to be possible in large and poorly staffed institutions. The designation of one staff member to take particular care of certain residents has led not only to greater consistency and better planned care, but also to the formation of deeper working relationships which have in themselves led to better care (Whitton, 1982).

In fieldwork, there has been a separate strand in the development of primary worker systems, particularly in multi-disciplinary child protection work. Clear responsibility for co-ordinating information and the activities of the other workers has been found a useful way to improve practice. The various models of 'care management' build on this (SSI 1991b).

From these two strands has come our concept of a primary worker as someone either providing personalised care to particular individuals or co-ordinating and monitoring the services of others, or both (Sackville, 1978).

A primary worker role spanning group care and work in the community presents logistical problems in most situations. Our focus is on the development of primary worker systems *within* residential and day-care units (cf Bromley, 1977; RCA, 1983; SCA, 1984).

A wide variety of names are used for systems of primary workers such as 'key worker', 'key person', 'link worker', 'special worker', 'named worker'. We have used the term primary worker (with a small 'p' and a small 'w') to indicate any of this range of functions. We have used this as a generic term, according to our own working definition.

A primary worker is:
A member of staff allocated the most significant professional role in relation to the care of a particular client.

The purpose of primary worker systems is to improve the quality of care provided to individuals by:

- improving the co-ordination of different elements of the assessment and care plan;
- providing physical care with greater consistency and more individuality, by having fewer numbers of staff intimately caring for any one client;
- ensuring that the needs of the individual are not lost amidst 'the group' or the organisation.

A primary worker system can be the key to creative care for individual clients (see for example, Taylor and Watton, 1983).

There are many varieties of primary worker systems. For example, in a family centre, one of the team is allocated as the main worker, including primary responsibility for liaison, recording and the relationship with the family, even though all direct work is undertaken on a co-working model. In a juvenile assessment centre, each child and family is allocated one primary worker, whether a teacher or a social worker. In a day centre, the professional day-care workers are allocated a number of clients for whom they provide counselling and oversee the care plan, as well as undertaking activities with various groups of members. In many homes for the elderly, the skills of care assistants as primary workers have been developed. In one home for the confused elderly each senior care assistant is designated as primary worker for a group of residents and a group of care assistants assist her in the primary worker responsibilities.

Our experience is that it is necessary to introduce a basic level of primary worker responsibilities in a residential unit before giving these staff greater responsibility for assessment and care planning. The situation in day care is comparatively straightforward in terms of developing basic professional staff in their role with individual clients. In Table 6.1 we have listed some of the tasks which might be allocated to care staff on a primary worker

Table 6.1   Primary worker tasks

Initial primary care tasks to be undertaken by a primary worker in a residential unit for the elderly: • bathing • shaving • nail care • daily recording – 'daily log' • clothing – tidying, marking, repairing (sometimes passed on to night care staff)
Further tasks which might be allocated to a primary worker in a residential unit for the elderly: • list shopping requirements (e.g. clothes, toiletries) • undertake shopping, sometimes with resident • birthday celebration • maintain resident file (assessment and care plan and monitoring) • liaison with relatives, clergy, doctor, etc • feedback to manager regarding client needs and wishes.

basis in a residential setting. We would not suggest attempting to allocate all of these tasks at once on a primary worker division of labour. It is generally better to begin by introducing one or two tasks to be redistributed on this basis, and then to progress to other tasks.

In Table 6.1 we have listed further tasks which could later be allocated to a primary worker. Again, we are suggesting an incremental development, rather than a flood. It will be seen that assessment and care planning are among the later tasks. The provision of physical care can then be more readily seen as a part of the care plan, just as the provision of a learning programme or therapeutic work would be.

Major task areas for the primary worker are shown in Table 6.2, including the full range from pre-admission to discharge.

For the manager of a unit, there are important issues to consider before setting up or developing a primary worker system. We have listed some of these in Table 6.3.

6.2   Supervision

The delegation of responsibilities for the assessment and care of individual clients requires a system for staff members to receive guidance and support and to account to the manager. This requires some measure of planned one-to-one supervision. This is normally called 'formal supervision' and it is often introduced in a residential or day-care unit in parallel with the development of a primary worker system.

Supervision is essential for good practice. Knowing that the line manager has reserved a space in his diary to sit down and talk about their work is experienced by most staff as supportive (Shulman, 1982). At this time, when the manager is taking a personal interest in what they have been doing, staff can bring him up to date on what has changed and seek comments about the situation.

In emphasising the need for planned one-to-one supervision to implement primary worker systems and comprehensive assessment and care planning, we do not wish in any way to undervalue the importance of other forms of supervision. In

Table 6.2   Primary worker care process

Major task areas of the primary worker in residential and day-care facilities
Pre-admission and admission: • assessment of match between client needs and services provided; • informing client and assisting in choice of services; • beginning to form working relationships; • settling in and transition of client administration.

Care process:	
Assessment	for specific provision (care, learning programmes, therapeutic work etc.);
Planning	co-ordinating work by others; liaison with outside bodies;
Implementation	relatives, other professionals, etc;
Evaluation	report writing and recording.

Discharge and after care: • facilitating transition: emotional, practical and relationship aspects; • evaluation and recording.

fieldwork settings, the fortnightly discussion between team leader and social worker about the current case-load is common. In residential settings, the informal supervision of 'management-by-walking-about' (see Peters and Waterman, 1988) is more common. Meetings of the whole staff group, and sub-teams within the total group may happen more frequently and fulfil some supervision functions (Atherton, 1986). Planned supervision, unplanned supervision, and management-by-walking-about are all important aspects of a manager's responsibility, as is the need for team meetings, other forms of group

Table 6.3   Developing a primary worker system

Points to consider in setting up a primary worker system:

Aims

- Do you have a clear aim for the primary worker system?
- How do the aims fit with the needs of the clients, staff, unit and wider agency?

Strategy

- Do you have a clear strategy for implementing a primary worker system?
- Have all appropriate people been consulted? (See section 6.3.)

Accountability

- Are the lines of accountability clear?
- Are the limits of delegated authority clear?
- Are confidentiality issues clear?

Staff

- What knowledge, skills, experience and qualifications do the staff have?
- Are particular needs, skills and interests known and if so, are they to be incorporated?

Allocation

- What criteria are to be used in allocating clients to staff, and in future changes of primary worker?
- Are client preferences or staff preferences to be considered?
- Who will deputise when the primary worker is on leave, sick, attending training, etc?

supervision, and ensuring that appropriate staff training is provided.

Traditionally, three strands to supervision are identified (Westheimer, 1977) as discussed below.

Accountability An opportunity for you to clarify your role and its boundaries, to seek decisions, to clarify which decisions you are enabled to take yourself, to consult, and check out proposed plans of work.

Support An opportunity for you to share the stresses and pressures of your work with your line manager and to plan ongoing support systems.

Development An opportunity to seek feedback on specific work which you have undertaken, and also to use the help of your line manager in developing your own knowledge and skills. This may involve the identification of your particular learning needs and seeking training or other work experiences to remedy this.

Although the responsibility for supervision rests with the supervisor, it is important that the supervisee takes on his own share of responsibility for the supervision sessions. Supervision is a two-way process, not one-way. A good supervisee can seek to arrange the date for the next supervision session. You should come with some items you wish to discuss. There is no reason why you should not open discussion about the sort of relationship which you and your supervisor are expecting to have. Finally, although it is the responsibility of the supervisor to ensure that the session is adequately summarised and future tasks clarified, you can take some initiative yourself as supervisee.

We see some system of one-to-one supervision as essential to support effective assessment and care planning.

6.3 Managing change

This book is about improving the quality of care given to individuals. Any improvement is a change. Most changes are threatening to at least some people. The introduction or development of assessment and care planning for individuals is a major undertaking, particularly where it involves a significant development of a primary worker system or a new supervision structure. This is a process which must be managed; giving staff a book to read is not enough.

Organisations, like living organisms, tend to settle to a steady state or 'homeostasis'. In seeking to develop better services, you are changing the steady state which exists. The primary question is: 'What change is acceptable now?'

We mentioned in Chapter 1 that the care planning cycle had parallels in management practice. It seems appropriate therefore that we should apply this framework to our discussion of the implementation of assessment and care planning, treating it as a management task.

Assessment

The first stage is to analyse the situation in the unit in relation to the proposed direction of change. One possible 'schedule' to aid information gathering about the organisation might be the 'Seven-S' Framework of Pascale and Athos (1982). The sort of questions which this suggests are shown in Table 6.4. A variety of other Organisation Development tools might also be used for this analysis.

Some staff can be extremely enthusiastic about change, while others may be quite resistant. You could anticipate a wide range of responses as illustrated in Figure 6.1. It may be useful to analyse the proposed plans in relation to the driving and restraining forces (Lewin, 1952). Having identified some of these forces (see Table 6.5), the task of the manager is to utilise the driving forces, and to minimise the restraining forces.

The manager's own enthusiasm will be important in motivating the staff group, but clarity about negotiable and non-negotiable elements may also assist. The vision of the staff as to 'where they are heading and why', might be enhanced by a visit to another establishment. Consultation with staff is required, and attentive listening to their points of view. The sequencing or timing of changes might be adapted in small ways which make the whole process more effective. It may be appropriate to utilise existing networks, for example discussion with informal

Table 6.4 Assessment of organisational functioning

Structure	What changes to the management structure are required? How will authority and responsibility be allocated? How will risks be managed?
Strategy	What development plans already exist? Have you a rationale for developing assessment and care planning, primary worker system, supervision? Will your priorities change? What are the benefits expected? What are the costs? What are the resources required? What time scale is anticipated? What side effects might there be?
Systems	What information systems already exist? Are there issues of access and confidentiality to be clarified? Are there significant gaps in the communication systems?
Staff	What new roles are being anticipated? How will the job definitions be affected?
Skills	What abilities and interests do staff have? What potential do they have? What are their training needs?
Style	What management style will be appropriate for initiating and managing this work? Are you sufficiently prepared yourself in terms of knowledge and skills?
Shared values	Is the function of the unit understood? Are staff committed to its aims? Does the strategy for development harmonise with the values in the organisation?

leaders or union representatives. Finally, a valuable question to ask yourself is: 'What is in it for them?'

Planning
Having developed an overall strategy, the next stage is to

Accept	Cope	Avoid	Deny	Sabotage

←———————————————————————→

Acceptance	Indifference	Passive resistance	Active resistance

Figure 6.1   A range of responses to changes

Table 6.5   Force field analysis

Driving and restraining forces in the implementation of individual care systems

Driving forces	*Restraining forces*
Increased job satisfaction	Fear of revealing 'survival mechanisms'
Clear relationship with clients and supervisor	Fears of favouritism
Staff development	Anxiety about revealing current skill level
Developing professionalism	Can't write
Increased responsibility	Boundary issues
Perceived client benefits	'There's no time'
	'It doesn't work'

develop an operational plan. This will include issues such as Who? What? When? How? A timescale should be detailed, allowing some slack for sickness or other eventualities. Resources need to be identified and clarified. A method for monitoring and evaluating the process must be established. Part of your assessment may have identified training needs of staff. Part of your planning may be to set up some training for them. There may be a training department within your organisation to assist in implementing a training programme. From our experiences, we would make the following simple points:

1 Training is best carried out as a joint exercise between managers and trainers.
2 In an organisation, train from the top downwards (i.e. the managers may need training *before* the practitioners).
3 Train people together who have to work together.

Implementation

Having an outline plan, the implementation phase involves working to that plan, and recording progress. Another task in parallel with this is to involve and inform other people as necessary.

Evaluation

The basic principles which we have suggested for evaluating care of individuals are transferable to a management context. The objectives identified at the start can be compared with what has actually happened. Both qualitative and quantitative changes can be examined as part of the evaluation of the total quality of service. Learning points for the next phase of the development can be collated. Staff can be congratulated for the progress that has been achieved. Change can be so threatening to people's sense of self-worth that even the most valuable and well-planned changes can bring anxiety. The positive staff comments may not be so loud as the fears; perhaps you can seek to make them louder!

Example: Introducing elements of assessment and care planning in a residential unit

The unit

Sanda is a thirty-two bed unit (not purpose-built and providing only dormitory-style accommodation) for male residents, many of whom are either registered as special care or have spent some considerable time in a psychiatric hospital.

The home had originally catered for difficult old men, many of whom had a nomadic background. Clothes were bought in bulk and even if some were ill-fitting, they were infinitely superior to those the residents were wearing on admission. Furnishings were adequate but uninspiring. The walls were gloss painted and the same colour throughout and the floor covering was linoleum.

Major changes have taken place over the past two years in the physical provision – carpets, curtains, wallpaper, furniture, etc. Attention now needs to be focused on the needs of residents as individuals, and on staff development.

Aim of the work

To begin to develop individual assessment and care planning by introducing a pilot primary worker system and staff supervision scheme to the unit.

Project objectives

1   To improve the care assistants' knowledge of, and skills relating to, specific aspects of assessment and care planning.
2   To introduce a primary worker system to the unit using two care assistants and six residents.
3   To introduce the practice of individual supervision of two care assistants.

continued

Introducing elements of assessment *continued*

Rationale for choice of project

1 Client's needs In the unit the residents' physical needs are well catered for but it would be a mistake to assume that in providing food, warmth, clothing, cleanliness and social activity we are meeting the individual needs of each resident.

The introduction of the primary worker system will mean that each resident will have a specific person to whom he can relate. The primary worker, by getting to know her particular resident and developing a closer relationship with him, should be able to offer choice, provide continuity of care and demonstrate sensitivity to individual needs.

2 Staff needs Staff require a better understanding of their role and responsibilities. This is particularly important since the role of the unit will gradually change from catering for the elderly to catering for younger mentally ill and mentally handicapped clients of 40 years and over. Staff must therefore develop new skills. This project will not directly seek to develop skills in work with these clients but will set up the basic structure.

Staff supervision would ensure accountability and would provide a vehicle for support and skill development. Through the primary worker system, care staff would become more involved in assessment of clients and in devising programmes of care. The fact that they are more involved should increase their motivation and job satisfaction.

3 Agency needs Supervision provides a vehicle for ensuring and monitoring standards of care. It can be an additional mechanism for effecting and monitoring agency policy development and change. A recent policy statement has required that all staff should receive formal supervision.

continued

Introducing elements of assessment *continued*

4 Own learning needs   I realised that as a Head of Unit there are areas in management skills which I needed to develop:

- To improve communication between management and care staff
- To give care staff the opportunity to develop their potential
- To delegate work to care staff and involve them in developing programmes of care for the residents
- To increase the information supplied to care staff
- To motivate staff
- To develop supervision skills

Knowledge base for the practice

For the purpose of developing knowledge and skills relating to supervision the following will be used: Atherton (1986), Shulman (1982), Westheimer (1977).

For the primary worker system: articles published in the various social work magazines and knowledge gained by staff in local units where the primary worker system is operating.

For developing management skills I will use the theory of authors including Whitton (1982), and Peters and Waterman (1988).

Project plan

Stage (I) Preparation: July–August

1 Consult with line manager, and professional mentor.
2 Discuss project with staff in the unit.
3 Begin relevant background reading.
4 Visit at least two other units implementing similar systems.

continued

Introducing elements of assessment *continued*

Stage (II) Planning: September

1 Select one senior care assistant, two care assistants, and six residents.
2 Arrange meetings with staff and residents involved to discuss project in some detail.
3 Plan:

   (a) Weekly supervision with senior care assistant;
   (b) Fortnightly meeting with senior care assistant and two care assistants (see 6).

4 Following discussion with staff, plan content of training and development sessions. These are expected to include topics such as assessment, programmes of care, primary worker, supervision, recording.

Stage (III) Implementation:
October–November–December

1 Planning and implementing a series of fortnightly development sessions with the senior care assistant and two care assistants. There will be at least six meetings commencing in October and ending in December. Each meeting will have two major parts: (A) teaching input and (B) group session.

   (A) Teaching input: basic topics as above, the exact content will depend on staff needs.
   (B) The group sessions will provide a forum for sharing ideas on implementation and an opportunity to discuss common problems and build morale.

2 Planning and implementing a series of weekly supervision meetings with the senior care assistant. The purpose of these meetings will be:

   (a) To provide support and discuss any problems which may have arisen in her supervision of the care assistants.
   (b) To discuss the content of the group sessions.

continued

Introducing elements of assessment *continued*

(c) To receive feedback on the progress of the care planning and primary worker system and on the views of other staff.

Stage (IV)   Evaluation: January

The project will be evaluated in terms of its objectives and the processes involved. Information will be gathered from staff, clients (through primary workers) and managers. A project report will be presented to my line manager by the end of January.

Resource implications

1 Line manager, professional mentor.
2 Senior care assistant and two care assistants.
3 Other staff in the unit.
4 Residents.
5 Library facilities.
6 Video and tape recorders.
7 Hand-outs and other teaching aids.
8 Clerical support.
9 Sitting-room.
10 Self.

Bibliography

Adcock, M. and White, R. (eds) (1985) *Good Enough Parenting: A Framework for Assessment*, British Agencies for Fostering and Adoption.

Argyle, M. (1972) *The Psychology of Interpersonal Behaviour*, Penguin.

Argyle, M. (1988) *Bodily Communication*, Methuen.

Atherton, J.S. (1986) *Professional Supervision in Group Care – A Contract-Based Approach*, Tavistock Publications, London.

Bailey, M.J.S. (1980), *Hampshire Assessment for Living with Others*, Hampshire Social Services Department.

Barrowclough, C. and Fleming, I. (1986) *Goal Planning With Elderly People – Making Plans to Meet Individual Needs. A Manual of Instruction*, Manchester University Press.

Bedford, A., Founds, G.A. and Sheffield, B.F. (1976) 'A New Personality Disturbance Scale', *British Journal of Social Work and Clinical Psychology*, **15**, 387–94.

Benson, J. (1987) *Working More Creatively With Groups*, Tavistock, London.

Biestek, SJ, Felix, (1957) *The Casework Relationship*, Unwin University Books.

Bluma, S., Shearer, M., Frohman, A. and Hilliard, J. (1976) *Portage Guide*, CESA **12**.

Brearley, C.P. (1982) *Risk and Social Work*, RKP, London.

Brechin, A. and Swain, J. (1987) *Changing Relationships: Shared Action Planning with a Mental Handicap*, Harper and Row.

113

Bromley, G. (1977) 'Interaction Between Field and Residential Social Workers', *British Journal of Social Work*, 7 (3), 285–99.

Carter, E.A. and McGoldrick, M. (1980) *The Family Life Cycle: A Framework for Family Therapy*, Gardner Press, NY.

CCETSW (1989) *Requirements and Regulations for the Diploma in Social Work*, CCETSW Paper 30.

Coulshed, V. (1991) *Social Work Practice – An Introduction*, Macmillan, London.

Crnic, K.A. Fredrick, W.N. and Greenberg, M.T. (1983) 'Adaptation of Families with Mentally Retarded Children: A Model of Stress, Coping and Family Ecology', *Am. J. Mental Deficiency*, 88 (2), 125–38.

Cunningham, C. and Sloper, P. (1978) *Helping Your Handicapped Baby*, Souvenir Press.

Department of Health (1988) *Protecting Children – A Guide for Social Workers Undertaking a Comprehensive Assessment*, HMSO.

Department of Health and Social Services (1983) *Personal Social Services Records – Disclosure of Information to Clients*, Circular LAC (83) 14 dated 24.8.83.

Department of Health and Social Services (NI) (1990) *People First: Community Care in Northern Ireland in the 1990s*, HMSO.

Doel, M. and Marsh, P. (1992) *Task Centred Social Work*, Ashgate, Aldershot.

Doll, E.A. (1936) *Vineland Social Maturity Scale: Revised, Condensed Manual for Direction*, Department of Research, Training School, Vineland, New Jersey.

Doll, E.A. (1953) *A Manual of Social Competence: A Manual for the Vineland Social Maturity and Scale*, Education Test Bureau, Educational Publishers, Minneapolis.

Egan, G. (1975) *The Skilled Helper – Model, Skills and Methods for Effective Helping*, Brooks Cole Publishing Company, Monterey, California.

Epstein, L. (1982) *How to Provide Social Services with Task-Centred Methods*, National Institute for Social Work, London.

Fahlberg, V. (1981) *Attachment and Separation*, British Agencies for Adoption and Fostering.

Feek, W. (1988) *Working Effectively – A Guide to Evaluation Techniques*, Bedford Square Press (NCVO).

Gilbert, P. (1985) *Mental Handicap – A Practical Guide for Social Workers*, Community Care – Business Press International.

Gray, B. and Isaacs, B. (1979) *Care of the Elderly Mentally Infirm*, Tavistock Publications, London.

Griffiths, Sir R. (1988) *Community Care: Agenda for Action*, A Report to The Secretary of State for Social Services by Sir Roy Griffiths, HMSO.

Gunzberg, H.C. (1969) *Progress Assessment Chart for Social and Personal Development Manual*, Volume 1. The Three Basic Forms, Volume 2. The Special P.A.C. Forms. SEFA (Publications) Ltd.

Gunzberg, H.C. and Gunzberg, A.L. (1987) *Learning Opportunities in Living Units for People with a Handicap*, SEFA (Publications) Ltd.

Gurel, L. et al. (1972) 'Physical and Mental Impairment of Function Evaluation in the aged: the PAMIE Scale', *Journal of Gerontology* **27**, 83–90.

Haley, J. (1976) *Problem-Solving Therapy*, Harper and Row, NY.

Herbert, M. (1981) *Behavioural Treatment of Problem Children – A Practice Manual*, Academic Press, London.

HMSO (1991) *Looking After Children: Assessment and Action Records:*
— (The Children Act, 1989)
— Guidelines for Users
— Children in Care: 0–1 year
— Children in Care: 1–2 years
— Children in Care: 3–4 years
— Children in Care: 5–9 years
— Children in Care: 10–15 years
— Children in Care: 16 years and over.

Hoghughi, M. (1980) *Assessing Problem Children – Issues and Practice*, Burnett Books.

Holden, U.P. and Woods, R.T. (1982) *Reality Orientation – Psychological Approaches to the 'Confused' Elderly*, Churchill Livingstone.

Holroyd, J. (1974) 'The Questionnaire on Resources and Stress: An Instrument to Measure Family Response to a Handicapped Member', *J. Comm. Psychol.* **2**, 92–4.

Hunt, J. and Hitchin, P. (1986) *Creative Reviewing*, Groundwork.

Hunt, P. and Young, A. (1984) 'Plainly Put . . .' in *Social Work Today*, 24 September 1984, 14–15.

Pascale, R.T. and Athos, A.G. (1982) *The Art of Japanese Management*, Penguin.

Pattie, A.H. and Gilleard, C.J. (1981) *Manual of the Clifton Assessment: Procedures for the Elderly*, Hodder and Stoughton, Kent.

Pease, A. (1981) *Body Language – How to Read Others' Thoughts by Their Gestures*, Sheldon Press.

Peters, T.J. and Waterman, R.H. (1988) *In Search of Excellence*, Harper and Row.

Pickles, T. (1987) *Working with Young People in Trouble – A Practical Manual*, Scottish Intermediate Treatment Resource Centre.

Pitman, E. (1984) *Transactional Analysis for Social Workers and Counsellors – An Introduction*, Routledge and Kegan Paul.

Priestley, P., McGuire, J., Flegg, D., Hemsley, V. and Welham, D. (1978) *Social Skills and Personal Problem Solving – A Handbook of Methods*, Tavistock Publications.

Reid, W.J. and Epstein, L. (1977) *Task-Centred Practice*, Columbia University Press, NY.

Reid, W.J. and Shyne, A.W. (1969) *Brief and Extended Casework*, Columbia University Press, NY.

Reith, D. (1988) 'Evaluation – A Function of Practice', 23–39 in Lishman, J. (ed.) (1988) *Evaluation*, second edition, Jessica Kingsley.

RCA (1983) *The Key Worker – A Social Report*, Horizon – Residential Care Association News in *Social Work Today*, 8 August 1983.

Rutter, M. (1967) 'A Children's Behaviour Questionnaire', *Journal of Psychology and Psychiatry*, **8**, 1–11.

Sackville, A. (1978) *The Concept of the Key-Worker – A Challenge to Traditional Thinking*, paper presented at a Study Day organised by the Residential Care Association, 10 May 1978.

SCA (1984) *The Key Worker Reviewed: A Working Paper*, Horizon – Social Care Association News in *Social Work Today*, September 1984.

Sheldon, B. (1988) 'Single Case Evaluation Methods: Review and Prospects', 40–57 in Lishman, J. (ed.) *Evaluation*, second edition, Jessica Kingsley.

Sheridan, M.D. (1982) *From Birth to Five Years: Children's Developmental Progress*, NFER-NELSON.

Name index

Adcock, M., 32
Ager, A., 33
Annis, H., 33
Argyle, M., 18
Atherton, J.S., 101
Athos, A.G., 104

Bailey, M.J.S., 33
Barrowclough, C., 34
Bedford, A., 33
Benson, J., 76
Biestek, F., 5
Bluma, S., 32
Brearley, C.P., 61, 87
Brechin, A., 3
Brody, E.A., 34
Bromley, G., 98

Carter, E.A., 32
Coulshed, V., 35
Cregan, A., 28
Crnic, K.A., 32
Cunningham, C., 32

Doel, M., 25
Doll, E.A., 32

Egan, G., 35, 74
Ellis, A., 75

Epstein, L., 25

Fahlberg, V., 32
Feek, W., 89
Felce, D., 32
Fleming, I., 34
Freud, S., 36, 76

Gilbert, P., 33
Gilleard, C.J., 34
Goldberg, G., 12
Gray, B., 34
Griffiths, R., xiii
Gunzberg, H.C., 33
Gurel, L., 34

Haley, J., 32
Herbert, M., 32, 33
Hipgrave, T., 32
Hitchin, P., 3
Hitchings, A., 33
Hoghughi, M., 32
Holden, U.P., 34
Hollins, S., 33
Holroyd, J., 32
Hunt, J., 3
Hunt, P., 80

Isaacs, B., 34

119

Subject index